THE QUALITY OF MERCY

Children in the Clay Square Mission, New Orleans. The Mission was maintained by students from the nearby Baptist Bible Institute. (Courtesy of the Southern Baptist Historical Library and Archives, Historical Commission, SBC, Nashville, Tennessee.)

THE QUALITY OF MERCY
Southern Baptists and Social Christianity,
1890–1920

Keith Harper

The University of Alabama Press

Tuscaloosa and London

Library of Congress Cataloging-in-Publication Data

Harper, Keith, 1957–
The quality of mercy : Southern Baptists and social Christianity.
1890–1920 / Keith Harper.
p.   cm.
Includes bibliographical references and index.
ISBN 0-8173-0814-8 (alk. paper)
1. Southern Baptist Convention—History—19th century.
2. Southern Baptist Convention—History—20th century.
3. Church work—Southern Baptist Convention—
History—19th century.   4. Church work—Southern Baptist
Convention—History—20th century.   5. Sociology. Christian
(Baptist)—History—19th century.   6. Sociology. Christian
(Baptist)—History—20th century.   7. Church and social
problems—United States—History—19th century.   8. Church
and social problems—United States—History—20th century.
9. Baptists—United States—History—19th century.
10. Baptists—United States—History—20th century.   I. Title.
BX6462.3.H37   1996
286'.132—dc20   95-37869

British Library Cataloguing-in-Publication Data available

For Johnnie and David

CONTENTS

Preface   *ix*

1. Reclaiming a Legacy: An Assessment of
Southern Baptists and the Social Gospel   *1*

2. Reaching the Dispossessed: Southern Baptist
Missions and Movement Culture   *15*

3. Preachers and Prelates: Southern Baptist Leadership
and the Emergence of a Social Ethic   *28*

4. Southern Baptists, Social Christianity, and Orphanages   *48*

5. Redeeming the Mountaineers: Southern
Baptists and Mountain Mission Schools   *72*

6. Of Leopard Spots and Ethiopian Skin:
Southern Baptists and Racial Uplift   *89*

7. Reassessing a Legacy: Southern Baptists,
Social Christianity, and Regional Context   *112*

Appendix I   *121*

Appendix II   *124*

Notes   *133*

Bibliography   *149*

Index   *165*

PREFACE

T HIS BOOK IS about southerners, or more precisely, Southern Baptists, and the ways they addressed social problems at the turn of the century. I chose *The Quality of Mercy* as my title because of Portia's now-famous lines from *The Merchant of Venice:*

> The quality of mercy is not strained,
> It droppeth as the gentle rain from heaven
> Upon the place beneath. It is twice blest—
> It blesseth him that gives, and him that takes.

We may rest assured that Shakespeare never met a Southern Baptist. Nonetheless, his description of mercy fits Southern Baptist attitudes toward society's dispossessed between 1890 and 1920, a fact that is frequently overlooked by contemporary scholars. That Baptists had a merciful attitude toward the needy is without question and deserves attention. Moreover, the quality of that mercy, what motivated and shaped it, also deserves exploration. Hence, the title.

Like any author, I hope this book enjoys a wide audience. Casual readers, therefore, may wish merely to skim chapter 1, which surveys pertinent literature on social Christianity and maps areas on which specialists in religious history disagree. Also, for those unaccustomed to Southern Baptist nomenclature, please be advised that minutes from state convention meetings, as well as those from the national convention, are usually referred to simply as "Annuals." I have followed that pattern in the notes, but not in the bibliography, where I used complete citations for each state.

On a different level, one of the most pleasant things about this project is acknowledging those who assisted me. When I was finishing my M.A. work at Murray State University, Huey G. Lawson, my thesis director, encouraged me to pursue a Ph.D. topic that was publishable. Thanks, Huey, for some of the best advice I ever followed. I owe a tremendous debt of gratitude to Ron Eller, Dan Smith, and Wayne Flynt, each of whom read several versions of this manuscript. I profited greatly from their advice, encouragement, and friendship. Lee Harding, my colleague in Mississippi College's English Department, read an early draft of this work and pronounced the grammar and style "okay"—for a historian.

Editorially, Malcolm MacDonald and the staff at The University of Alabama Press have been exceptionally helpful. In addition to his other kindnesses, Malcolm secured three readers for this manuscript who helped me rethink some of my early conclusions. I may not have followed all their recommendations, but I appreciate their thoughtful reflections, and I believe their suggestions strengthened this work. Nancy Roseberry carefully copyedited this manuscript with a professional precision I envy. Thanks, Nancy. Additionally, Jonathan Randle and Barbara Mauer both made "noteworthy" contributions, and Kerri Stanley saved me from "innumerable" difficulties. Likewise, John T. Williams, Rich Holl, George Ellenberg, Todd Estes, and Dan Lykins offered good-humored encouragement, as did my colleagues in the History and Political Science Department at Mississippi College.

No scholar can do research without libraries, librarians, and archivists. I am no exception here, and I want to thank Paul Debusman at the James Petigru Boyce Library at Southern Baptist Theological Seminary, Louisville, Kentucky, for his timely assistance. Bill Sumners, archivist for the Southern Baptist Historical Library and Archives, Nashville, Tennessee, was also very helpful and very encouraging.

Special thanks is also due to the Southern Baptist Home Mission Board and the Sunday School Board, who graciously allowed me to reproduce the materials found in Appendixes I and II, respectively. I thank Chrystelle Thames of the Mississippi Baptist Children's Village, who secured permission to use two photographs from that institution's early days. I also thank the Southern Baptist Historical Commission. In addition to granting permission to use most of the photographs in this book, the Commission also awarded me a study grant that facilitated my work. Additionally, I received generous financial assistance from The Project on the Governance of Non-Profit Organizations at the Center on Philanthropy, Indiana University, Purdue University, Indianapolis, Indiana, which allowed me to pursue this project over the course of an entire summer.

Finally, I wish to thank those to whom this book is dedicated, namely, my wife, Johnnie, and son, David. Johnnie typed every draft of this manuscript and scrutinized each page with a perfectionist's eye.

She also encouraged me and believed the book was doable even when I had my doubts. Without her, I would not have completed the project. And David—let's just say that he is the *best* son in the world. He is daddy's "helper man," and what a help he is! David has made our lives richer than we ever hoped or imagined. I am truly thankful this project is finished, but in Johnnie and David I have personal, loving reminders that some things in life are infinitely more important than others. For that I am most thankful.

THE QUALITY OF MERCY

I

RECLAIMING A LEGACY
An Assessment of Southern
Baptists and the Social Gospel

SOUTHERN BAPTISTS have a rich and diverse history, much of which, understandably, has been tied to southern history as a whole. Unfortunately, it has also been tied to negative southern stereotypes, the worst of which depict the South as a backward region devoid of cultural value and beyond social redemption.

Of course, these images do not accurately portray southern culture. Nevertheless, they have influenced the way certain scholars view southern evangelical attitudes, especially those regarding social issues. In *Origins of the New South*, C. Vann Woodward noted that early twentieth-century American Christianity was characterized by increasing church unity, an increasingly liberalized theology, and a growing emphasis on Social Christianity. "Yet," he lamented, "one searches vainly for important manifestation of any one of these tendencies in the annals of Southern Christendom. Indeed, there is evidence that the current in the South ran counter to all three tendencies."[1]

Like Woodward, many historians argue that the Social Gospel was a phenomenon that stayed well north of the Mason-Dixon line. Two of the earliest studies of the Social Gospel movement expressed this sentiment and greatly influenced subsequent scholarship. Charles Howard Hopkins's *The Rise of the Social Gospel in American Protestantism, 1865–1915* and Henry F. May's *Protestant Churches in Industrial America* are still standard works on American Social Christianity. Neither study successfully defined exactly what the Social Gospel was, but Hopkins's 1940 study argued that the Social Gospel resulted from the impact that industrialization and the technological revolution of the late nineteenth and early twentieth centuries made on American society. Hopkins was also the first to observe that the Social Gospel was indigenous to North America.[2] May's work was published nine years after Hopkins's and examined the thought of five major denominations regarding social issues. After closely scrutinizing the Presbyterians, Methodists, Baptists, Congregationalists, and Episcopalians, May concluded that as industrialization increased throughout the nineteenth century, the major denominations chose to defend the status quo rather than answer the challenge posed by contemporary social critics. He attributed this to the fact that many denominational leaders equated the laws of classical economics to the laws of God. Nevertheless, May found three distinct strains of Social Christianity. Conservatives, he argued, advocated mild societal reform, whereas radicals wanted to overthrow "the system" peacefully. Moderates, those whom May described as "Social Gospelers," wanted to modify society drastically, but they were unwilling to sacrifice the capitalist order.[3]

Despite the insight of these works, they are not without flaws. Hopkins, for example, correctly observed that the Social Gospel was associated with the rise of industrialization, but he failed to place the movement within its broader social context. Moreover, neither May nor Hopkins paid any attention to southern religious sources, especially denominational newspapers, and thereby omitted a substantial portion of nineteenth-century American religious thought.

Other studies have tended to follow May's and Hopkins's lead. In *The Social Gospel in America,* Robert T. Handy maintained that the Social Gospel was indigenous to North America and that it manifested itself in at least three different forms. Handy's study was unique, however, in several ways. First, his work was a comparative biography of Richard T. Ely, Walter Rauschenbusch, and Washington Gladden, three men actively involved in the Social Gospel. Second, and more important, Handy maintained that the Social Gospel movement was "shaped by patterns of thought and action that had long been characteristic of American Protestantism."[4] Indeed, the Social Gospel may have been new in the early twentieth century, but its ideological roots were much older.

These works by no means exhaust the impressive historiography of the Social Gospel movement, but they are instructive. They suggest that the Social Gospel resulted from the twin forces of urbanization and industrialization and that the Social Gospel was not a monolithic entity. Moreover, they also suggest that the heart of the Social Gospel was a liberal theology that de-emphasized creedal Christianity in lieu of a more socially oriented expression of vital piety.

Two of these factors are antithetical to southern society prior to World War I. The early twentieth-century South was overwhelmingly rural and did not experience industrialization or urbanization in the same manner as the North. Additionally, the South is the home of the so-called Bible Belt. Southern religion of the early twentieth century was decidedly conservative and fundamentalist in its understanding and interpretation of the Bible. Thus, southern religion has its own distinct features.[5]

Many scholars have noted these and other differences between the North and the South and concluded that the South had no Social Gospel movement. The questions they seem to pose are several: If the Social Gospel arose as a result of urbanization and industrialization, influences that, presumably, scarcely touched the South, how could the South claim to have a Social Gospel? If the South tended to reject theological liberalism in lieu of theological converservatism and Biblical literalism, how could anything even remotely resembling a Social Gospel movement develop within Dixie?

Several scholars have studied social reform as it relates to southern churches and have concluded that the Social Gospel was a northern phenomenon. In 1964, Kenneth K. Bailey's *Southern White Protestantism in the Twentieth Century* examined the white South and its dominant religious groups, especially the Baptists, Methodists, and Presbyterians. Bailey was among the first to examine the social interests of southern religious groups. His study suggested that between 1900 and 1915, southern evangelicals had no Social Gospel, but Southern Baptists, Methodists, and Presbyterians were both increasingly aware of social injustice and becoming more willing to speak out against it. But, he added that at the turn of the century southerners were scarcely aware of social needs "beyond blue laws and Prohibition."[6]

Shortly after Bailey's work appeared, Rufus Spain published a pioneering study titled *At Ease in Zion: A Social History of Southern Baptists, 1865–1900*. Spain, a social historian who studied the Southern Baptists from 1865 to 1900, concluded that this period was characterized by resistance to change rather than a direct confrontation of social problems as they existed. Spain argued that Southern Baptists failed to develop a high degree of social consciousness for a variety of reasons. First, the Social Gospel was initiated by scholarly clerics in the face of dramatic social upheaval in the North. By contrast, southerners tended to be "common people" with neither extensive educational backgrounds nor an appreciation of the subtleties of Social Gospel leaders and their arguments. Also, the Social Gospel was new and innovative. Since Baptists saw themselves as God's keepers of orthodoxy, they were suspicious of religious activities that were not directly associated with preaching the Gospel and personal salvation. Spain also observed that Baptists practiced a highly congregational type of church polity, so even if a Southern Baptist minister favored the Social Gospel, his congregation might not. Finally, Spain noted that southerners during this era had an extreme "southern" outlook. They were in no hurry to overcome those regional prejudices that had spawned the Confederacy and resisted Reconstruction. The Social Gospel's link to northern churches, Spain suggested, was sufficient grounds for many southerners to reject it.[7]

True, the South had not experienced the same social changes that industrialization had created in the North. Nevertheless, Spain conceded that, in reality, Baptists did develop a degree of social awareness. In fact, many southerners admitted that social service was a viable aspect of Christianity. As Spain put it, "While openly refusing to admit any deviation from tradition, Baptists nonetheless modified their denominational program to accommodate in many practical ways the new emphasis on socialized religion."[8]

In 1972, John Lee Eighmy expanded upon this argument in *Churches in Cultural Captivity: A History of the Social Attitudes of Southern Baptists*. Eighmy maintained that the Social Gospel movement in the North really had affected southern churches, most notably by challenging long-held southern assumptions regarding the church's proper mission. As more ministers and laypersons saw the church as an institution with a stake in social justice, they became involved in social issues. But, he noted, even though Social Christianity was more widespread than commonly assumed, southern churches by no means exhausted their possibilities in the area of social benevolence. This was because they were tied too closely to old southern cultural folkways, social conservatism, and local church autonomy that made social activism a voluntary matter. They were captives of their own culture, Eighmy argued, and this narrow commitment to regionalism and provincialism rendered southerners unable to comprehend the larger picture of social injustice, much less to act constructively upon it.[9]

Others have either denied southern Social Christianity on an extensive scale or lumped all religious benevolence under the specter of mere charity. Samuel S. Hill, Jr., has written numerous works that have in one form or another reiterated this thesis. In *The South and the North in American Religion*, he maintained that the South had a unique religious system, and he based his analysis on three assumptions. First, he noted that one of the key features of the southern religious distinctiveness was that southern churches failed to develop a social ethic. Second, he maintained that religion is an "independent variable" that exerts causative force and is not merely a reaction to other forces such as economics or politics. Finally, he disputed Eighmy's contention that southern churches were in "cultural captivity." Rather, southern churches were instrumental in *shaping* southern culture.[10] Consequently, there could be little room for the Social Gospel if religion's causative forces were acting upon churches devoid of a pronounced social ethic.

In *Southern Churches in Crisis*, Hill maintained that one of the greatest problems southern evangelicals faced was their preoccupation with individual salvation. This preoccupation had not, however, kept them from developing a genuine social concern. "Although the southern church has never devoted its energies to the redemption of the social structures, and certainly warrants no identification with the 'social gospel' tradition," he said, "it has not been blind to the relation between the Christian faith and a number of social currents and responsibilities."[11]

In a slightly different vein, James J. Thompson, Jr.'s, *Tried As by Fire: Southern Baptists and the Religious Controversies of the 1920s* examined Southern Baptists and the controversies that dogged them in the 1920s. Although this work is not primarily dedicated to an analysis of Social Christianity, Thompson nevertheless noted that southerners were generally opposed to the Social Gospel because they associated it with theological liberalism. Also, World War I had cast a new light on Social Christianity by questioning the assumption that humanity's nature was basically good. Additionally, the fundamentalist controversy made Baptists more aware of the liberal tone of the Social Gospel. Southern Baptists feared that excessive social concern would destroy the "spiritual core" of their religion.[12]

Finally, John B. Boles has cast his lot with those who deny that a Social Gospel movement developed in the South. In a recent article, Boles agreed with Samuel S. Hill that the central theme of southern religion has been individual salvation, not social concern. He conceded that southern churches frequently engaged in charitable endeavors. Nevertheless, Boles insisted that because Baptists, Methodists, and Presbyterians dominated the southern religious landscape at the turn of the century, only the "very fringes of Southern Protestantism," such as the Methodist Episcopal Church, South, and certain radical clerics, were able to transcend parochial southern religious tendencies and produce meaningful social critiques.[13]

Yet, despite these assessments, considerable doubt remains that southern Christians failed to participate significantly in addressing their contemporary social problems. Neither do they prove that Social Christianity in the South was mere charity. Each of these scholars readily concedes that southern churches actively participated in a variety of social issues ranging from implementing Prohibition to enforcing Sabbath laws. They also agree that such limited forays into the social arena do not constitute participation in anything resembling a Social Gospel movement.

This traditional perspective has been challenged by a growing number of scholars who see Social Christianity as a much more vital force than previously acknowledged. By far, the most impressive challenge to the old guard has come from those who have examined women and religion of the late nineteenth and early twentieth centuries. These scholars have investigated such issues as temperance, prohibition, and antilynching legislation and found that southern women used their various churches and missionary agencies to initiate social change.[14]

Yet southern women were not the only southerners who displayed social concern. For the past twenty years Wayne Flynt has argued that both male and female southerners consistently addressed social issues. Their commitment was neither concentrated within any single denomination nor confined to any particular issue. Flynt, himself a Baptist, devoted considerable attention to the Southern Baptists, especially in Alabama. He noted that between 1900 and 1914 Southern Baptists in Alabama frequently advocated social change, especially if it would aid the southern economy. They also championed numerous other causes such as child labor reform, health care, and education. While it is true that not all southerners were willing advocates of the Social Gospel and Southern Baptists were decidedly Fundamentalist in their understanding of the Bible, this did not prevent their confronting societal challenges. In fact, Flynt argued that the leading advocates for reform in Alabama were theological conservatives who interpreted the Bible literally.[15]

In addition to the Baptists, Flynt has also studied Southern Presbyterians in relation to Social Christianity, especially in Appalachia. Again he argued that southern social concern was strong in both urban and rural areas. Walter L. Lingle, Pastor of the First Presbyterian Church of Atlanta, Georgia, for example, energetically advocated social reform in both rural and urban America ranging from uplifting Appalachians and blacks to championing women's rights. This drive for social reform ultimately revealed internal divisions within the Presbyterian ranks. Some objected to the rising tide of ecumenism, arguing that such measures were tantamount to sacrificing Presbyterian distinctiveness. For others, however, the desire to effect social change stirred an interest in reuniting the two wings of American Presbyterianism.[16]

John W. Storey has also questioned the thesis that Social Christianity was all but nonexistent in the South. In *Texas Baptist Leadership and Social Christianity, 1900–1980*, Storey challenged a number of widely held notions regarding the role of Social Christianity. First, he disputed Eighmy's contention that southern social awareness and concern stemmed from the Social Gospel in the North. Storey argued that though Texas churchmen were aware of men like Walter Rauschenbusch and Josiah Strong, their social concerns arose independent of direct northern influence. Second, Storey argued that there were differences between the Social Gospel in Texas and its northern counterpart. For example, whereas the Social Gospel in the North was directly associated with theological liberalism, which deemphasized humanity's inherent sinfulness and stressed brotherhood, Social Christianity in Texas remained staunchly conservative and emphasized personal sin and redemption in Jesus Christ.

Additionally, Social Gospel activists advocated religious intervention into society as a means of securing social and institutional changes that would, in turn, alleviate such problems as substandard wages and child labor. Texans, at least until the Depression, remained committed to individual salvation as a cure for all social problems. They believed that society improved only as individuals improved. Personal salvation, therefore, was at least the best way to begin making society better.

Finally, Storey disputed both Eighmy's and Spain's arguments that the South resisted change because of its rural traditions. Using Texas as a model, Storey noted that the Lone Star State had enjoyed significant urban growth throughout the twentieth century. Nevertheless, it still had a decidedly rural cast, and Texas Baptists had retained a commitment to social issues, especially Prohibition and gambling. Urbanization, he concluded, was only part of the story of Social Christianity in Texas. The other factors he saw that influenced social concern within Texas Baptist ranks were the editorship of the *Baptist Standard*, a denominational newspaper based in Dallas, influential urban pastors with their own social concerns, executive positions within the Southern Baptist bureaucracy at the state level, and the faculty at Southwestern Baptist Seminary. Thus, a group of denominational elites with a deep interest in such social issues as alcoholism, race relations, and family life used a variety of platforms to relay this concern to Baptist laypeople.[17]

One may wonder how scholars such as John B. Boles and Samuel S. Hill, Jr., could apparently disagree with others such as Wayne Flynt and John Storey. How may one account for such differences in perspective? There are a number of possible explanations. In a perceptive assessment of Southern Baptists and social reform, Flynt noted that both Southern Baptists and their critics have too quickly assumed that a certain "religious homogeneity" has always existed among Baptists that allowed for no diversity of thought on either theological or social issues. Also he noted that earlier scholars implied that sincere social reform could only rise from theological liberalism. Since Southern Baptists were reluctant to embrace such liberalism, it was simply not possible that a Social Gospel movement would develop in the South. Moreover, Flynt maintained that many scholars have fallen into the "consensus historian trap." That is, they have emphasized continuity in Baptist thought rather than heeding the various voices of protest. Consequently, a broad range of Baptist thought and action has been overlooked.[18] If Flynt is correct, could the same be said for other southern religious denominations?

Scholars dismissing Southern Baptist commitment to social issues may also have erred in using too narrow a range of sources. Since Southern Baptists meet annually as a "convention," it is tempting to use Convention minutes at the national level as a barometer for all denominational activity. Yet social issues, especially at the turn of the century, were more likely to be discussed at the state and association levels. Historians must look here if they seek insight into the ways Baptists addressed social issues.

Yet another possible explanation for the differences between these scholars may simply be a semantic one. What exactly is the Social Gospel? Henry F. May used the term "Social Gospel" to describe a particular school of social theory that arose from the teachings of men such as Washington Gladden in the early twentieth century. He distinguished the Social Gospel from "Social Christianity," which, as he saw it, was a more general term implying "Christian solutions" to social problems.[19] Yet, this concept of the Social Gospel may miss the point. As Sidney E. Mead has observed, the Social Gospel was never incorporated into any new, independent organizations and spawned no new denominations. Mead also argued that the Social Gospel rested on no single theological mind-set. Previous studies have argued that the Social Gospel hinged on a liberal theology that blunted the concept of original sin in favor of human beings as innately good. But according to Mead, the theologies associated with the movement were diverse and highly individualistic. "It was in reality," Mead said, "a movement in the denominations looking for theological roots."[20] Robert Handy has likewise noted that the Social Gospel was a diverse movement that included radical, conservative, and moderate groups.[21]

If the Social Gospel defies definition, those scholars who maintain that the South experienced nothing akin to genuine social reform face several problems. At a practical level, if the Social Gospel has no real consensual definition, but most scholars willingly concede that southern churchpeople voiced concern over societal ills, how can one argue that a Social Gospel was not evident in southern churches? Moreover, no one has assessed the impact that the Social Gospel made on northern churches. If the Social Gospel was a narrow, highly individualized ideology confined to a small number of clerics and their congregations, was it truly representative of most northern Christianity? If it was not, is it fair to castigate southern churches for what did not, in fact, exist in the North?

The paradigm suggesting that the Social Gospel is a strictly northern, urban phenomenon is likewise open to several problems. First, to assume that the Social Gospel sprang from such forces as immigration, urbanization, and industrialization creates a bias against any evidence that does not fit that particular pattern. The assumptions and implications are clear. If the South did not experience immigration and urbanization as the North did, there must be no Social Gospel. Yet between 1890 and 1920 the South underwent considerable change resulting from industrialization. Textiles, mining, lumbering, and in some quarters, steel making were booming southern industries. To date, however, no one has assessed either their impact on southern churches or the church's response.[22]

Additionally, by assuming that the Social Gospel arose from a liberal theological perspective, scholars unnecessarily limit their perspective. It is absurd to think that only liberal theologians desired to ease human suffering. As Storey and Flynt have noted, the most active participants in Social Christianity in Texas and Alabama were theologically conservative. If that is true, exactly what role did theology play in forming one's worldview?

Clearly, one of the keys to understanding southern religious response to human misery lies in defining the Social Gospel. Hopkins argued that it arose from industrialization and urbanization. Mead argued that it defied any sort of theological or institutional definition. Rather, Mead said that the Social Gospel movement represented the reaction within denominations to the idea that some planned socioeconomic controls should be exercised to curb the excesses of nineteenth-century American capitalism. Even this, he noted, ran counter to the thought that had built the "machine" that needed curbing.[23] Storey and Flynt maintain that southerners, particularly Southern Baptists, were vitally involved in social issues, whereas Boles and Hill affirm that no Social Gospel movement existed in the South. Obviously, they cannot both be correct.

The debate over whether the Social Gospel ever manifested itself in the South may go on indefinitely. It may be time to aim the question in a new direction. If scholars agree that southern churches addressed social issues, even if minimally, what exactly did these churches do and what fundamental assumptions did they make?

This study attempts to answer these questions by focusing on Southern Baptists between 1890 and 1920. Robert D. Linder has suggested a threefold distinction between Christian social concern, action, and ministry that may be useful for this work. According to Linder, social concern is "a general interest in society's problems," particularly those issues touching on interpersonal relationships, social issues, and explicit Bible commandments. He equates social action with "organized effort at any level—personal, nonpolitical, and political"—seeking to bring prevailing socioeconomic conditions more into conformity with Bible principles. Finally, he suggests that social ministry addresses Christian efforts, individual or collective, to assist "those individuals harmed by adverse social conditions."[24] Linder summarizes the essential differences between social ministry and social action by saying, "Social action is more concerned with the causes of harmful social conditions; social ministry is more concerned with their effects."[25]

Between 1890 and 1920, Southern Baptists displayed social concern, social action, and social ministry. They saw their primary duty as evangelism, but this did not thwart their desire to assist society's dispossessed. From their calls for Prohibition and "blue laws" to their establishment of orphanages and mountain schools, Southern Baptists demonstrated that they were strangers neither to social action nor to social ministry. Hence, this study will use the term "Social Christianity" to describe the ways Baptists addressed contemporary social problems. This usage of Social Christianity is not dramatically different from John W. Storey's usage in *Texas Baptist Leadership and Social Christianity, 1900–1980.* Storey, however, used the term to distinguish southern, rural, evangelism-conscious Texas Baptists from northern Social Gospel thinkers, who tended to be urban liberals proposing to reform society institutionally.

Because Baptists saw their primary duty as evangelism, Social Christianity represents their synthesis of evangelical outreach with social concern, as defined by Linder. They believed institutional reform was superficial and insisted that the only way to create a better world was by changing its people's character. They sought to convert souls, and in so doing, change society by furnishing it with better, that is to say converted, people. By combining social concern with the impulse to evangelize the world, Baptist leaders enlisted rank-and-file church members to donate their money and focus their attention on perceived southern socioeconomic problems. This approach enabled Baptists to build a variety of new institutions, including hospitals and settlement houses. It also encouraged ministers to address social issues with an almost noblesse oblige spirit. Consequently, Baptist social ministries generally tended to be conservative and paternalistic. Nonetheless, Baptists made remarkable efforts to help the needy despite the economic hardships of the day.

Taking this argument one step further, the Social Christianity that Southern Baptists practiced between 1890 and 1920 must be understood within its cultural context. In the original preface to *Churches in Cultural Captivity*, Eighmy wondered how one might account for the different approaches northern and southern Baptists took in addressing social problems. "Part of the answer lies in regional and organizational differences," he concluded, "but that hardly solves the problem."[26] Eighmy may have dismissed regional differences between the North and South too hastily. Joel Williamson has argued that at the turn of the century, the South was an "organic society." As such, southerners placed particular emphasis on "placeness."[27] According to Williamson, "In the organic society, people would know their places and function and those of others around them. They would govern themselves in those places with keen awareness of the approval of others within their circle."[28] As the various components of southern society found their "place," internal dissension was not possible.[29] Between 1890 and 1920, Baptists believed they could assist everyone's search for place. Spiritually, this implied conversion. Physically, Baptists chose to rely on established institutions such as the church and family to meet all personal and societal problems.

Finally, what made the period between 1890 and 1920 a time of pronounced Social Christianity for Southern Baptists? There are two answers. First, these three decades mark a time when Southern Baptists were becoming increasingly conscious of their own denominational identity, as well as of their own place within southern society. It was also between 1890 and 1900 that Populism made a profound impact on

The "Good Will Center" was similar in function to settlement houses. This one was in Louisville, Kentucky. (Courtesy of the Southern Baptist Historical Library and Archives, Historical Commission, SBC, Nashville, Tennessee.)

the South. For Southern Baptists, however, Populism was less significant for its politics than for its particular "movement culture," which emphasized democracy, egalitarianism, and mutual self-help. These tenets well suited Baptist polity, which emphasized local church autonomy and democratic church membership. Second, Baptists were ready to meet the challenges of a new century thanks to the legacy of the Second Great Awakening. In a thought-provoking article, Donald G. Mathews suggests that the primary characteristics of the Second Great Awakening were unity and organization that resulted in new "institutional forms" and standardization of "what had once been spontaneous."[30] The Southern Baptist Convention was formed in 1845 with two agencies dedicated specifically to evangelism: the Foreign Mission Board and the Domestic and Indian Mission Board, which later became the Home Mission Board.[31]

Throughout the antebellum period, considerable Baptist thought centered on slavery.[32] Once slavery was no longer an issue, Baptists faced new challenges, including race relations, education, and, of course, evangelism. But, rather than creating entirely new institutions to address such problems, Southern Baptists turned once again to existing institutions, most notably local churches and the Home Mission Board, to find answers to the "New South's" socioeconomic problems. Moreover, when Baptists did build new institutions, such as orphanages, they were centered around church and family life. Hence, the seeds sown in the Second Great Awakening sprouted, grew, and blossomed for Baptists between 1890 and 1920.

The combined impact of southern culture and Baptist polity helped create a unique response to social problems. Southerners had deep social concerns. Their Biblical literalism compelled them to take seriously social admonitions from the Bible. Their emphasis on traditional values sought personalized, individual answers to far-reaching problems. As Southern Baptists faced a rapidly changing socioeconomic scene at the turn of the century, they sought, to borrow Dewey W. Grantham's phrase, to "reconcile tradition with progress."

2

REACHING THE DISPOSSESSED
Southern Baptist Missions
and Movement Culture

"Can two walk together except they be agreed?"
Amos 3:3

Between 1865 and 1890, the United States, particularly the northern states, witnessed breathtaking industrial and economic expansion. It was likewise an important time for Baptists in the South. While northerners faced industrialization's benefits and curses, southerners tried to dig themselves out of the Civil War's rubble and rebuild a once-vibrant economy. Still, southerners also benefited from many technological advancements, especially the typewriter and linotype, which Baptists used to enhance one of the more prominent features of Baptist life, the denominational newspaper.[1] These newspapers gave Baptists a forum for expressing both doctrinal and social opinions.

Some Baptist historians have suggested that this period was also a time of increasing Baptist "self-awareness." Robert A. Baker writes of the Convention "claiming its birthright," and H. Leon McBeth notes that from 1845 to 1900 Northern and Southern Baptists were "going separate ways."[2] In fact, McBeth writes, "Despite several efforts at continuing cooperation, and even talk of reunion, the chasm seemed wider in 1900 than in 1845. However, each group had vastly multiplied its benevolent work, as if provoking one another to good works. Not just their isolation from each other, but the impact of different socio-economic forces shaped Baptists in the two regions into separate molds."[3]

The implications of this self-awareness are significant. Southern

Baptists perceived themselves to be different from northern Baptists in doctrine and practice. They saw many of their problems as being different, distinctively southern. They also believed they had the solution to these problems. Baptists expressed concern for issues from immigration and labor to temperance and gambling. But rather than turning to politics to effect social change, Baptists relied on personal evangelism through missionary activity. Their reasoning was simple. They believed that creating a better society depended upon supplying that society with better people. Baptists, therefore, sought to convert individuals who would, in turn, apply Christian ethics to their personal and public/business lives. Between 1890 and 1920, Southern Baptist social criticism hinged not only upon the assumption that better societies were built on better people but also upon a set of cultural assumptions inherited from the Populists. Between 1890 and 1920, Baptists used missionary activity to synthesize these assumptions and forge a social ethic that became the backbone of their Social Christianity.

In the early 1890s, the People's Party mounted a serious challenge to America's traditional two-party system. The Populists advocated numerous reforms, ranging from free silver and the subtreasury plan to secret ballots and the direct election of United States senators. Numerous works have explored Populism's diverse contours, but Lawrence Goodwyn's *Democratic Promise* is particularly instructive. He identifies a grass-roots sentiment, a "movement culture," that spawned the People's Party. Certain distinct, identifiable features of this movement culture coalesced with numerous Baptist tenets. First, there was a sense of individual self-worth and self-respect. Southern farmers had suffered greatly from the humiliation of crop lien, a vicious feature of post–Civil War southern agriculture that locked its victims into a debt-credit cycle from which few escaped. In the late 1880s and 1890s, midwestern and southwestern farmers were scarcely better off than the debt-ridden southern farmers.[4] Goodwyn argues that Populism was an agricultural reaction to the unfairness, exploitation, and degradation of both the crop lien and the American economic system. "At bottom," says Goodwyn, "Populism was, quite simply, an expression of self-respect. It was not an individual trait, but a collective one, surfacing as the shared hope of millions organized by the Alliance into its cooperative crusade."[5]

Another element of the movement culture was a willingness on be-

half of Populists to work together with others for the group's benefit. This spirit of mutual self-help was manifested in cooperative
stores. Most farmers believed they were charged excessive rates on
the commodities they purchased. Consequently, they tried to bypass
the "middleman," or local merchants, by forming their own stores
and buying goods directly from manufacturers and selling directly to
farmers. That such stores failed is unimportant. The point is that
farmers demonstrated a willingness to work together in a cooperative
venture to ease their economic woes.[6]

The heart of the movement culture was a collective sense of purpose. Goodwyn argues that Populists shared a desire to stand united.
They had a plan for making American society more democratic, and
they were determined to see it implemented. Their spirit and determi-
nation were so fervent that some scholars detect religious fervor in
Populist rhetoric. Moreover, Populists openly borrowed religious tech-
niques in their meetings, particularly the "camp meeting." These
meetings were especially popular in July and August, the lull before
harvest. They would come by the thousands to sing, pray, share mutual
woes, and discuss ways to improve their lot. Such meetings also reclaimed agrarian "backsliders," or those who had grown lukewarm,
toward People's Party goals. Of course, it was also a time to solicit new
converts.[7] Sometimes, it was impossible to distinguish between religious zeal and political partisanship. As one historian notes, "Amid
the fervor of the camp meeting, reform and religious faith blended into
a single righteous cause."[8]

If self-worth, self-reliance through cooperation, and a collective
sense of purpose are the salient features of the Populist "movement
culture," the emergence of a leadership corps and an emphasis on education may be identified as "movement corollaries." While these corollaries are perhaps not specific elements of the movement culture, they
are, nonetheless, important features. For example, Goodwyn notes
that S. O. Daws and William Lamb, two early Populist leaders, had
been victims of crop lien. Hence, even though they rose quickly to
national prominence, they were still common folk at heart who could
readily sympathize with their constituents. Furthermore, Populist
leadership displayed an almost fanatical commitment to education.
Each Alliance had its own lecturer, and any group meeting was an opportunity to preach the gospel Alliance style.[9]

The extent to which political Populism was a mass democratic movement may be debatable. The point here is neither to assess Goodwyn's concept of Populism nor to suggest that all Southern Baptists were Populists. In fact most Baptists at the turn of the century remained loyal Democrats. Nonetheless, Goodwyn's movement culture describes an intriguing cultural context for the late nineteenth-century South. The movement culture from which Populism sprang was a grass-roots folk movement that could have manifested itself in a variety of ways. This movement culture was perhaps better suited to religious aims than political aims. Politics notwithstanding, even Goodwyn notes that once attained, the movement culture "opens up new vistas of social possibility, vistas that are less clouded by inherited assumptions."[10]

The Populist movement culture of the late nineteenth century provides valuable insight into the way Baptists addressed social problems. Although Populism failed as a political movement, the movement culture's salient features of individual self-respect and self-worth, the willingness to work cooperatively, the collective sense of purpose, and the emergence of an elite that advocated education found religious expression in the Southern Baptist Convention. That is, Southern Baptists practiced a form of church government that dovetailed nicely with this movement culture's main tenets.

The Populist objective of a democratized American society can be seen in microcosm in any Baptist congregation. Each Baptist church functions as a democratic, autonomous body in which all members are equal. Local churches arrange their own worship services and have absolute control over who is admitted into their membership. There is no age limit regarding membership, but the Baptist rejection of infant baptism requires candidates for church membership to be old enough to acknowledge personal faith in Christ.[11] The function of a church is twofold. On the one hand, churches are for worshiping God. Here again, each Baptist church establishes its own times for worship services. On the other hand, churches exist for service to God. Such service includes a variety of functions, from teaching and evangelization to community service, especially local benevolence.[12]

While Baptist life focuses on the local church, it is not limited strictly to that capacity. Southern Baptist churches form associations at the district level. There are no specific criteria for defining what constitutes an association. Sometimes the churches within a given county form an association. If the population is sparse, two or more counties may form an association. In large metropolitan areas, churches within the city limits may constitute an association. Regardless of size, these associations meet annually. Baptist life at the associational level usually focuses on missionary activities. Because the churches that comprise the association are autonomous, resolutions passed at the annual meeting are nonbinding. As E. C. Routh notes, "At present, the average Southern Baptist church conceives the association of Baptist churches with which it is affiliated to be an organization through which it voluntarily cooperates with other member churches for special mission ministries within the associational area, and from which it gains the values such an organization can contribute to the churches in the manifold areas of their interest and cooperation."[13]

Beyond the association is the state convention. As with other Baptist bodies, state conventions are sovereign within the bounds of their constitutions. State conventions meet annually and stand as "the body through which Baptists provide for themselves institutions and programs of promotion and missions, which are related to a local area but which cannot succeed without the support of a constituency larger than that of the district association."[14] Most Southern Baptist social concern is expressed through the associations and state conventions. One scholar notes, "The state bodies, from the beginning, stressed foreign missions, the enlargement of district associations to reach destitution in the state, Sunday schools, the publication of Baptist papers, pastoral support and ministerial education."[15]

After the state conventions is the Southern Baptist Convention. The convention meets yearly, and it is perhaps not going too far to suggest that the "convention" is similar to a giant business meeting where the various boards, agencies, and commissions that work on behalf of Southern Baptists have an opportunity to report on their previous year's activities. The convention also provides a forum whereby delegates, whom Southern Baptists call "messengers," discuss issues pertaining to Southern Baptists. Resolutions are nonbinding, and participation in convention programs is voluntary.[16]

Stated succinctly, turn-of-the-century Southern Baptist polity emphasized minimalism. Baptists actively sought only the organizational structure necessary to implement their programs, especially missions. Consequently, the absence of a hierarchial form of church government and Baptist insistence on democracy and autonomy within local churches forged a set of circumstances whereby Baptists thrived within the Southern cultural context. That is, Baptists offered a form of religious service that seemed somehow appropriate for its cultural setting and appealed to many.

If sharecropping and crop lien had robbed southerners of their self-worth, church was an excellent place to reclaim one's esteem. This is especially true when one considers the universality of the Christian message: Christ died for sinners. Thus, the furnishing agent might be a harsh man, but God loves people—even sharecroppers. While it is true that other Christian groups preached God's love and redemption through Christ, the fact that Baptist churches were democratic bodies was not lost on those who joined.[17]

Populists called for mutual cooperation, and Baptists responded with volunteerism. They received into their membership only those who joined of their own accord. Churches voluntarily participated in Southern Baptist missionary activities. In fact, Baptist organization at the local, state, and national levels was based entirely on voluntary participation.

Additionally, as the nineteenth century closed, Baptists grew vitally concerned with education. Southern Baptist Theological Seminary in Louisville, Kentucky, was establishing its academic reputation at that time, and before 1920 Baptists had a second seminary, Southwestern Baptist Theological Seminary, Fort Worth, Texas, and The Baptist Bible Institute, New Orleans, Louisiana. They also built schools in the southern mountains and maintained an impressive network of colleges. Likewise, they had a leadership corps of individuals with whom they could identify. Many were Civil War veterans, some chaplains. All were sympathetic to southern socioeconomic problems, and nearly all had a rural upbringing.

If Baptists were seizing opportunities to expand education, they never forgot that their primary goal was evangelism. By 1890, they already had a leadership corps dedicated to Southern Baptist causes, especially to education and missions. Many of these leaders provide excellent examples of the movement culture's most salient features, namely, cooperation and volunteerism. For example, in 1907 E. Y. Mullins, President of Southern Baptist Theological Seminary, wrote of a "crisis" in Home Missions. He said the South's most pressing issues were directing rapid material development, mobilizing the large number of Baptists in the South, and developing a greater missionary zeal within Baptist ranks. Mullins feared that material development would outpace spiritual development. Baptists stood at a crossroads, and Mullins believed that his brethren could "seize and hold the South for all time to come"—if they would seize the opportunity.[18]

Of course, to seize the opportunity meant expanding missionary efforts. The concept of missionary activity marks the movement culture's heart as concerning Social Christianity and Baptists. Evangelical missions gave Baptists the collective sense of purpose that united them in a quest not only to save souls but also to right certain societal wrongs. They wanted to redeem the world, and to this end they rallied around missionary activity. Nevertheless, Baptists did not confine their missionary zeal to the pulpit. Between 1890 and 1920, Southern Baptists built numerous institutions ranging from schools and orphanages to hospitals and settlement houses. They preached the gospel, and they also sought to relieve human suffering.

Expanding missionary activity required leadership and commitment from local churches to provide adequate financing. That Southern Baptists had adequate leadership is indisputable. Even before Mullins had spoken of the Southern "crisis," the editors of *Our Home Field*, the official magazine of the Home Mission Board, noted, "Never before were Southern Baptists more united in their purpose to take this Southland for Christ and they were never so well equipped for the holy work."[19] They also said the South was a Baptist "paradise" and claimed that more than three fifths of all Baptists lived in the South. Moreover, Baptists were becoming more affluent and influential. They noted the only problem was that most Baptists were no better developed spiritually than southern resources were developed materially. The solution was simple. They called for more contributions, enhancing the building and loan fund to assist new churches, a greater emphasis on "urban work," and greater emphasis on ministering to immigrants.[20]

Missionary zeal as a driving influence behind social activism may be analyzed from two perspectives. From an obvious religious perspective, Baptist missionary activity was designed to get people converted and, ideally, listed on membership roles in local Baptist churches. Yet there was more. This perspective also maintained that converted individuals would apply Christian ethics to their lives. William Louis Poteat illustrated this point by arguing that early twentieth-century socialism suffered from its failure to see moral evil as "the root of all social unrighteousness." He also said, "The present-day impulse toward amelioration of social conditions, by whatever name it may be called, is distinctly a Christian impulse, and it is of the highest importance that it find its proper channel and roll its undivided volume forward upon its task."[21] Poteat, like other Baptists, believed he knew how to accomplish this task. "Briefly stated," he said, "the method of Jesus is regeneration by an inward spiritual ministry, social righteousness through the vital, contagious leaven of individual righteousness. He renews all social life at its source in the individual human heart, and trusts the new life to take on the external embodiment which is appropriate to it."[22] Poteat concluded that individual conversions that prompted new social awareness would eventually lead to the creation of a "Christian public opinion." This "Christian public opinion" would ultimately, in his view, lead to the exclusion of all opinions not compatible with it.[23]

Baptists expected conversion to produce fundamental changes in individuals that would, in turn, lead to moral behavior and compassion for the less fortunate. An editorial in the January 1914 edition of *The Home Field* lambasted socialism. It also conceded that society was growing more complex and demanded greater social ministry on behalf of Baptist churches. The crux of the matter hinged on Christians, not political systems. "Ideal social conditions," the writer noted, "can never be brought about without ideal men and women to make those conditions. The only dependable approximation toward high ideals in human life and character is that which comes from the touch of God and the human soul."[24] Further delineating the difference between socialism and Christian missions, the writer observed that socialism sought environmental changes in order to save people, whereas Christianity sought to save people who would save the environment.[25]

Southern Baptist missionary zeal, therefore, was not confined to conversion. Viewed from another perspective, Baptists had a good idea of how conversion should affect individuals and the type of fruit it would produce. They believed that social stability through law and order was one such fruit. In 1909, William J. McGlothlin, a professor at

Southern Seminary, noted that the southern mountains and the western frontier desperately needed help and that Southern Baptists needed to respond before the opportunity was gone. "An educated society in the mountains and a settled and fixed society on the frontier," he argued, "lie in the not distant future."[26] McGlothlin doubtless saw evangelism as a means to achieving social stability. Here again, the pattern was the same. McGlothlin believed that once converted, individuals would adopt a set of Christian ethical principles. These principles would lead to brotherly love and instill a sense of reciprocal obligations one for another. Ostensibly, the result would be less crime and greater social stability.

Mountain feuding is a good example of how Christianity was supposed to produce order and social stability. C. S. Gardner agreed with McGlothlin that social chaos was a problem, particularly in the mountains. Yet he identified the basic problem not as "excessive individual bloodthirstiness, but a very backward stage of social development."[27] He quickly added that missionary work would cure the problem, especially Christian education, which would provide mountaineers with "higher ideals" and displace their moral "darkness" with Christian "light." Gardner believed Christianity could replace a "clan spirit" with "the consciousness of universal human brotherhood and the man across the mountain is seen and felt to be a brother as truly as the man who dwells in the same valley."[28]

A. E. Brown was even more explicit. In 1911, he argued that in only twelve years mountain schools had contributed to an improved mountain morality. He said, "The moral tone has greatly improved, crime has lessened, feuds have disappeared, respect for law inculcated."[29] Additionally, he noted that mountain converts had a strong temperance sentiment.[30] Clearly both A. E. Brown and C. S. Gardner saw social implications beyond conversion. Both saw conversion as a means of uplifting mountaineers, providing them with a new sense of dignity.

Another fruit that missionary zeal supposedly fostered was patriotism, or more specifically, an antisocialist spirit. As early as 1894, J. S. Dill warned his fellow Baptists that liquor, immigration, and labor posed serious social problems. He believed liquor was a "monster that slays the noblest and best . . . a 'vampire' sucking the lifeblood of the nation."[31] He believed immigrants posed numerous problems ranging from Russian nihilism and German beer to French, Irish, and Italian

Catholicism, all of which he believed "must be subdued, or else they will subdue us."[32] He believed Christianity could solve these problems by redeeming the alcoholic through love, assimilating the foreigner through the "molding influences" of "our religion," and solving labor disputes through brotherhood.[33]

Clearly, Baptists believed that evangelizing immigrants would lead to their assimilation. Most believed true Christianity would also discourage socialism among discontented Americans. "Socialism is alien in America," warned a 1907 editorial in *Our Home Field*. "It is a part of the import baggage of unAmerican immigrants."[34] The editorial also admonished its readers that immigrant religious practices were "already laying their despoiling hands on the American and Christian Sabbath."[35] Nevertheless, the editors were confident the gospel could turn the tide.

Southern Baptists believed that the same gospel that converted Americans could convert immigrants and have similar social effects. For immigrants, conversion was a call to become not only a Christian but an American as well. They were to divest themselves of any cultural traits foreign to American folkways and become "true" Americans. Conversion for those already American was likewise a summons to patriotism. Southern Baptists were expected to stand as moral examples to the world, especially with regard to keeping the "Christian Sabbath" and obeying the law.

Finally, Baptists tended to believe that evangelism and the missionary impulse would produce social changes that would foster social cohesion. Essentially, Baptists believed that conversion made each individual more "community conscious." This community consciousness may best be described through example. In assessing the impact of Baptist work on mountaineers, A. E. Brown believed the quality of mountain life had improved. His evidence was that many mountaineers had remodeled their homes, adding conveniences that reflected "advanced ideas of home life."[36] The Reverend R. R. Acree made a similar observation. Acree served as a mountain evangelist, and on one occasion his preaching led to the conversion of a certain Jenkins family. Acree encouraged Mr. Jenkins to build a larger, better house and to let his children attend school. Moreover, he told Jenkins that God expected him to do everything he could to make his home "glorious." Acree soon left the mountains for an unspecified time, but he ultimately returned to visit the Jenkinses. To his delight, Acree discovered that Jenkins had built a "two-story cottage." They invited Acree to stay with them, and he overheard Mr. Jenkins's remark, "Won't he be proud of the house? Lord; he don't know; he don't know what he had done for us, but we know."[37]

Determining exactly what Acree had done for the Jenkins family is not easy. They were obviously pleased with their faith and thankful that Acree had preached the gospel to them. Yet by comparing Acree's story with A. E. Brown's assessment of mountain Christianity, one sees that both men wanted Christianity to make more than a spiritual impact. Their references to housing are significant. Neither explained exactly what constituted "advanced" ideas of home life, but it may imply two things. It could be that they saw a need for each family member to have adequate space. It could also indicate a willingness to be more hospitable. Acree stayed with the Jenkins family for some time. Such openness to strangers indicates a heightened awareness of Christian social obligation.[38]

In addition to identifying Social Christianity's desired effects, Baptists also expected people in local congregations to get involved in social issues. The chief reason for this was that Christianity itself produced social unrest. C. S. Gardner articulated this principle clearly when he said, "A thorough understanding of his [Christ's] principles will create social unrest, discontent with conditions as they are, because it makes more obvious the unrighteousness and unbrotherliness in them, just as the plumb line reveals the lack of straightness and uprightness in a wall."[39] He quickly added that the social discontent that sprang from Christianity was constructive and sought to apply Christ's ethics to socioeconomic life. He argued that most people did not dread social agitation for better social conditions, but rather the hatred and violence that often accompanied social agitation. He believed Christianity would solve this problem. "The iniquities and evils which Christianity reveals," he said, "can be remedied only as men can be brought to practice Christianity. Men in their business methods and ideals, in their political programs and policies, must be governed by the principles of Jesus."[40]

The question was, How can church members fulfill their obligation in such an ambitious undertaking? One writer proposed a three-step approach: the preacher, the church, and the State and Home Mission

Boards.[41] He admonished preachers to deliver sermons that would be "social forces" heralding a gospel not for "disembodied spirits" but for flesh-and-blood human beings living in an "organized society." He called on churches to jettison the notion that churches were a "Noah's Ark" for the elect. He said, "The church must grip its own community."[42] He called on the State Boards and Home Mission Board to work together to coordinate this missionary work.

Finances were essential to the missionary effort to christianize the South, and church members provided financial backing through their contributions. Such offerings, however, were not always limited to currency. There are examples of individuals and churches that donated goods to assist missionary efforts, especially benevolent efforts. In April 1908, for example, *Our Home Field* briefly mentioned "boxes" being sent to mountain schools. Although the article never explained what the boxes contained, it is reasonable to assume that local churches had received such articles as shoes and clothing for children attending the schools. Another possibility is that the boxes contained food or staples such as flour. The point is that offerings were not always monetary. Ministers encouraged people to give what they could, and this sometimes resulted in unusual gifts. Nevertheless, it also allowed people to donate to a cause in which they were taught to believe—missions. By not insisting upon strictly monetary gifts, Baptist leaders allowed even the poorest church members to get involved in systematic giving.

Some evidence suggests that Southern Baptists became increasingly stronger and self-conscious as a denomination in the late nineteenth century. One question remains: If Southern Baptists constituted a self-conscious group between 1890 and 1920, what are the social implications?

On the one hand, Southern Baptist commitment to social issues tended to focus on those areas for which they could find a Biblical mandate. The book of James, for example, admonishes its readers to care for widows and orphans. Baptists built institutions to care for orphaned children and rested confidently that in so doing they served their Redeemer. The same is true of hospitals, settlement houses, and the like. Moreover, since Baptists emphasized local church autonomy and since limited funding prohibited extravagance, most socially benevolent missionary activity was limited to rather small areas. There were exceptions. After 1890, orphanages and hospitals tended to be state projects, and there was never an effort to bring them under the Convention's control.

On the other hand, Southern Baptists never abandoned their commitment to individual salvation. They believed their primary function was to preach Christ's gospel. Yet, this did not preclude social ministry. It did, however, shape its parameters. Southern Baptists, especially the leadership corps, tended to be an optimistic lot who genuinely wanted to see changes in society. Such changes would occur only via individual conversions. They believed that effecting change through politics from without was decidedly inferior to changes wrought from within. They believed that conversion to Christianity precipitated holy living, which in turn created better citizens. They maintained that this was the only way to initiate lasting, worthwhile changes in society. Moreover, these elites got individuals involved in social ministry through missions. Such willingness to assist social ministry indicates that social consciousness was not limited to the Southern Baptists' upper echelons. In fact, true to typical patterns of Progressive Era reform, Baptist benevolence began at the local level and worked its way upward.[43]

Between 1890 and 1920, Baptists believed that they were changing society as souls were being saved. Since society seemed willing to change, Baptists enjoyed an enviable advantage. They appealed to a people who already had a collective sense of individual self-worth, a willingness to assist others, and a sense of purpose. The movement culture that spawned Populism also provided a backdrop for Baptist benevolence and a platform from which they could address contemporary societal issues. They required no sophisticated theological justification for social action; they simply needed a clearly articulated purpose. Yes, preaching the Gospel would convert the non-Christian world, but for those unwilling to finance missionary endeavors beyond "mere preaching," the sluggish economy and mass deprivation posed convincing arguments to help the needy as missionary undertakings. This was a role with which Southern Baptists became increasingly comfortable through the first two decades of the twentieth century.

3

PREACHERS AND PRELATES
Southern Baptist Leadership and
the Emergence of a Social Ethic

"And it shall come to pass afterward, that I will pour out my spirit upon all flesh; and your sons and your daughters shall prophesy, your old men shall dream dreams, your young men shall see visions"

Joel 2:28

Between 1890 and 1920, Southern Baptist leaders began calling for increased concern for social justice and ministries geared to help the needy. These individuals constituted an elite within the convention, men who shaped polity and actively served as leaders in Baptist agencies such as the Home Mission Board.

One of the best ways to see this concern is by examining denominational leaders who contributed to Baptist thought and polity between 1890 and 1920. These key leaders helped lay the groundwork and furnish the collective identity for contemporary Southern Baptists. This leadership corps was composed of men who came from different backgrounds and served Southern Baptists in a variety of forms, yet they shared important characteristics. They manifested a strong tie to the South as a distinct region; they were especially concerned with southern social problems; and they anxiously anticipated a new socioeconomic order in the South.

Education was a priority with these Baptist leaders. In fact, education was a central feature of southern Progressivism, especially among Baptists. In 1913 the Southern Baptist Convention declared, "God believes in education."[1] A casual reading of the Convention *Annuals* at both the state and national levels reveals that Southern Baptists expressed increasing concern regarding education between 1890 and 1920. That same 1913 Convention, for example, also maintained that each state within the bounds of the Convention should have "at least one absolutely first-rate college."[2]

The turn-of-the-century South was ripe for a boom in education, and churches—particularly Southern Baptist ones—tried to meet this challenge. Their plans were grandiose; their resources were minimal. Nonetheless, Kenneth K. Bailey noted that of the 26,237 students attending southern colleges, universities, and technical schools in 1900, some 13,859 attended church-related institutions.[3]

Southern Baptists expanded their educational enterprises between 1890 and 1920. It is noteworthy that they established the Southwestern Baptist Theological Seminary in Fort Worth, Texas, and the Baptist Bible Institute in New Orleans, Louisiana, to complement the Southern Baptist Theological Seminary in Louisville, Kentucky, which had been established in 1859. These seminaries are important because they assumed the responsibility of educating Southern Baptist ministers. If the faculty in these seminaries were committed to addressing social problems, it is reasonable to assume that they transmitted at least a portion of this concern to their students who in turn may have shared it with their congregations.

The Southern Baptist Theological Seminary was founded in 1859 in Greenville, South Carolina. Owing to financial difficulties in post–Civil War South Carolina, the Seminary moved to Louisville, Kentucky, and classes began there in September 1877, just as Reconstruction was officially ending.

James Petigru Boyce is usually identified as the Seminary's founder, and his educational philosophy rested on three premises. He believed that ministers should have access to theological instruction regardless of their educational background; otherwise, ministers would be inadequately prepared to meet their congregation's needs. He also believed that students who were capable should have access to special courses that would best develop their talents because Baptists needed their own thinkers. Finally, he insisted that each professor at the seminary subscribe to a doctrinal statement, thereby preserving doctrinal integrity.[4]

While the seminary was clearly an institution dedicated to educating pulpiteers, it was much more than that. Before long, the seminary established a reputation for addressing social problems. On September 27, 1886, Dr. John A. Broadus, who had been with the seminary since its inception, wrote a newspaper article for the *Courier-Journal* in which he denounced lynching as a great evil. He also noted that associated with lynching were two other problems, namely, scorn from poor whites and alienation of law-abiding blacks. He observed that black people differed widely among themselves due in part to the various relations they had had with white people while they were in slavery. He chided his fellow southerners for allowing the practice to go unchecked and warned, "If we continue to tolerate lynching we lead these better Negroes to think that we are the enemies of all their race. We alienate the better class from the support of justice and government and civilization."[5]

With this spirit in mind Southern Baptist Theological Seminary hired Charles Spurgeon Gardner in 1907 to teach homiletics and Christian sociology. Gardner, who taught at the seminary until 1929, was instrumental in alerting his fellow Baptists to the gospel's social implications.[6] For example, on November 13, 1912, Gardner relayed his concern for social issues to the General Association of Baptists in Kentucky. Recognizing that southern society was changing, he said, "It is impossible for the churches to remain unaffected by the universal social ferment, and it is the part neither of wisdom nor of faithfulness to their spiritual function for them to assume an attitude of indifference toward it."[7]

Gardner called for action at three levels. First, he challenged churches to provide what relief they could for the needy by themselves. Seeing that most churches had limited financial assets, Gardner called for intradenominational cooperation. Citing success in financing missionary endeavors and praising the example of Baptist orphanages, Gardner saw no reason that benevolent activities could not be expanded. He favored institutions such as hospitals, especially in larger cities, settlement houses in poorer districts, and special agencies to address labor-related issues. Finally, he called for interdenominational cooperation to achieve more general social reform. He said that Baptist involvement in the temperance crusade had taught them that they could unite with those of different theological persuasions without compromising their own beliefs in order to fight social evils. Surely, he believed, this work could be expanded.[8]

In 1914, Gardner articulated his ideas on Christianity and social issues in *The Ethics of Jesus and Social Progress*. His observations merit close scrutiny. Conscious of the socioeconomic problems that industrialization had produced, Gardner argued that the solution to the problems was a religious one. This was especially true in light of the "growing recognition" that the contemporary social ferment presented one of the greatest challenges Christianity had ever experienced. "Thus," he concluded, "the new science of social relations has opened new and rich fields of thought for the students of Christian ethics and theology, who are beginning to feel that one of the great religious tasks of this generation is the proper correlation of Christianity and social science in their common task of guiding society toward the goal of universal righteousness."[9]

Gardner argued that the kingdom of God to which Jesus referred in the New Testament had both spiritual and secular implications. He believed this kingdom would be manifested upon the earth in its fullest glory at some future time. Until then, however, earth's societies were in an evolutionary process—the kingdom was coming. Moreover, the church was vital in bringing about new social orders. Unfortunately, its efforts were often squelched by those outside the church or ignored by those within the church. Neither of these factors absolved the church from its God-given role as agent of social change.[10]

According to Gardner, the kingdom of God had three methods at its disposal by which it could implement social change: construction, destruction, and reconstruction. The process he labeled construction involved dissemination of ethical ideals upon which people were to build their lives. The church, obviously, was to play the leading role in construction by espousing and implementing Christ's ethical teachings. Additionally, construction involved establishing benevolent institutions such as hospitals, orphanages, and asylums to care for society's dispossessed and disadvantaged. The process he labeled destruction involved legal action aimed at destroying those institutions and practices that appealed to one's baser nature. For example, Gardner was a prohibitionist and supported legal measures to curb the alcohol industry. True to the spirit of Progressivism, destruction also involved ending political corruption. Finally, the process he labeled reconstruction involved the reorganization of those institutions necessary for social life under more Christian influences.[11]

In spite of Gardner's appeal for Christian social amelioration, he repeatedly noted that ultimately all change had to come from within individuals rather than through external mandates. For example, Gardner maintained that Jesus had neither strived for nor insisted that the world's people should work for full social equality. Yet he differentiated between what he deemed good and bad social systems, and he tried to answer two popular arguments. On the one hand, he dismissed those whom he called hyper-Calvinists, who maintained that all features of the social system were ordained by God. On the other hand, he dismissed social Darwinists who argued that the existing social structures were the product of natural process. Both positions had some element of truth, he said, but neither correctly reflected the optimal social system. As Gardner explained it, people were endowed with moral features that distinguished them from the animal world. Thus, if a social system exploited and dehumanized its population, people were to change the system through love and mutual respect.[12]

Because all were not equal, those with superior endowments were to serve those less fortunate. Gardner stressed this as a "Kingdom principle" and left it to others to figure out exactly how it should be implemented. Nevertheless, his remarks on wealth are significant. According to Gardner, wealth was not necessarily bad. Only when people sought wealth for selfish purposes did it become an evil. He argued that those who had wealth should use it for the advantage of others. It was only in a life of service to others that people would find their ultimate fulfillment and that social tensions would be eased.[13]

If the church were to play the leading role in demonstrating Christ's ethics, it is also clear that Gardner saw the family as an institution with a kindred mission. To him the family was society's most vital institution.[14] Yet the rapid changes that society had experienced under industrialization had shaken family stability. Nevertheless, he maintained that the family could thrive, indeed must thrive, in an industrial society, but there were three requisites. First, both husbands and wives had to recognize the mutual responsibilities of their marriage covenant. This meant they were to serve each other. Second, they were to keep their marriages free from sexual infidelity. Third, they were to raise their children with the proper moral and physical care. In so doing they would provide themselves and their children with security and set an example for others to follow. Gardner also suggested three principles for upholding marriage as distinct from the family. People needed to have their religious faith revitalized. That is, couples needed to see their marriage as a religious and not a purely secular obligation. He also advocated laws that would regulate divorce, as well as laws that would make it more difficult for people to get married, especially the insane, neurotics, those infected with "social diseases," and those for whom marriage simply would be a mistake. Finally, he said that by establishing fair economic conditions and equitable living standards for all, marriages would not face the economic stress that so often led to divorce.[15]

Ironically, on the eve of World War I, he closed his work with these words:

> A world-consciousness is developing; and corresponding to it a world-consciousness is crystallizing, and it is crystallizing around the fundamental principle of the ethic of Jesus—universal good-will. War—and every form of conflict between men—is more and more coming under the prohibition of this conscience; and the particular form of patriotism which has its genesis in the unfriendly opposition of nations is growing weaker, while that form of it which is tributary to the passion for humanity is growing stronger as the spirit of the Son of man spreads through the hearts of men and draws them into a universal and ethical brotherhood.[16]

While C. S. Gardner was calling for fundamental social changes, George Broadman Eager, his colleague at Southern Baptist Theological Seminary, was also calling for churches to assume a more active role in administering social justice. Eager was Professor of Biblical Introduction and Pastoral Duties at the Seminary from 1900 to 1920.[17]

Much like Gardner, Eager believed that Christianity had paid too much attention to individual conversion and too little attention to interpersonal social relations. He said, "The social ideals of Jesus, his vision of a kingdom of love and righteousness, of sonship and brotherhood, of a new and renewing influence permeating the mass like leaven, ruling and controlling in all human relations—in short, of a redeemed humanity and a reorganized society—these have been neglected and kept in the background."[18]

Eager quickly added that ministers and earnest Christians were coming to see that the ethical standards of God's Kingdom on earth demanded that righteousness, fair-dealing, justice, and brotherly love needed to be manifested. "The problem of life," he observed, "used to be the problem of the individual; now it is the problem of society in its organized form. One hundred years ago the family was the little world; now the world is fast becoming one vast family and government is paternal."[19] It was, therefore, incumbent upon everyone to work for the well-being of others.

In effecting social change Eager admonished his students to put their priorities in the correct order, as ministers should never forget that their primary duty was tending to spiritual matters. Even optimal social conditions could not make people into Christians, and he warned that reformation was not synonymous with redemption. Nevertheless, he also warned his students that their success would be limited so long as their congregation was hungry. "There is little hope," he said, "of a successful Sunday School or Gospel service in a crowded, unsanitary, vice-breeding tenement. Moreover, it is well-nigh hopeless to reach the laboring man with the Gospel so long as he believes that he is the slave of the capitalistic class, made up so largely of those who call themselves 'Christians,' and that his wretched condition is largely due to the apathy of the churches."[20] Eager then challenged his students not to target any particular class for specific action but to deal with all classes and thereby elevate the entire community.[21]

While Southern Baptist Theological Seminary's professors were challenging their students and fellow ministers to consider and act constructively on contemporary social problems, Texas Baptists were building the denomination's second seminary. In 1908, Southern Baptists established the Southwestern Baptist Theological Seminary in Fort Worth, Texas. Benajah Harvey Carroll was its guiding force. Carroll had been instrumental in promoting religious studies at Baylor University in Waco, Texas. In fact, in 1901, Baylor officially established a theological department, but when Baylor's president, S. P. Brooks, later opposed expanding the department, Carroll eventually established Baylor Theological Seminary in 1905. Three years later the university and the seminary separated because of internal friction, and the fledgling theological school became Southwestern Seminary.[22]

Carroll was a recognized leader among Texas Baptists and frequently served as a revivalist. Many of Carroll's sermons were reprinted and distributed as tracts and booklets. Perhaps his most noteworthy literary contribution, however, was his seventeen-volume *An*

B. H. Carroll, Founder of Southwestern Baptist Theological Seminary. (Courtesy of the Southern Baptist Historical Library and Archives, Historical Commission, SBC, Nashville, Tennessee.)

Interpretation of the English Bible. Originally delivered as lectures to his seminary students, his *Interpretation* is salted with stories, personal reflections, and sermonettes that provide valuable insight into Carroll's thought.[23]

Carroll was concerned about ministerial education for many reasons. He believed that the Southwest needed well-trained, orthodox ministers. Yet sending young Texas ministers to Louisville posed a couple of problems. It was a long, expensive trip that few could afford. Moreover, those who were able to attend Southern Seminary frequently stayed in Kentucky. It is also possible that Carroll was not satisfied with the administration at Southern Seminary.[24]

Whatever his reasoning, one thing is clear: B. H. Carroll was suspicious of, even hostile to, sending young ministers to seminaries north of the Mason-Dixon line. Carroll had served the Confederacy during the Civil War, and he may have retained some lingering sectional hostility. Another possible explanation was Carroll's contempt for the so-called higher critical methods many northern seminaries had begun using. At one point he warned his students, " . . . you can understand what I mean when I said woe to the South, where the people have the views of sound doctrine, when it sends its preaching implements to a northern radical-critic grindstone in order to put on point or edge."[25]

On another occasion Carroll lectured from the book of James on the subject of fault-finding in others. Using what he called "The New England Conscience" as a negative example, he criticized writers from New England who smugly wrote about their pure consciences:

> It has always been a strange conscience to me. That conscience said, "For you to persecute us is a sin. It is all right for us to persecute you." That conscience said, "The sin of the Southern slavery will not let us sleep, but our own sectional sins put us to sleep." That conscience said, "It was an awful thing for South Carolina to threaten only to nullify a Federal law, but it was patriotism for us to nullify many times, actually a Federal law." . . . That conscience said, "Southern secession is treason, but it is patriotism for us to originate and teach the doctrine of secession as the best thing for ourselves." . . . That conscience pilloried Gen. Early for burning one town, but it glorified Sheridan for burning all the homes in the Shenandoah Valley and Sherman for burning a section seventy miles wide from Atlanta to Savannah.[26]

Of Carroll's sectional sentiments there can be no doubt.

Yet Carroll was also profoundly interested in social issues. When Texas layman R. C. Buckner established the state's first Baptist orphanage, B. H. Carroll was one of its original contributors and was among its first assistant supervisors.[27] Carroll also expounded his social concern to his students at Southwestern. In discussing Jesus' statement that His followers were both salt of the earth and light to the world, he noted, "I say today, in the Name of the Lord Jesus Christ, that but for the humble, God-fearing men and women in any state, in any century, in any town, it would rot."[28] Of course, Carroll maintained that Christians should lead exemplary lives, but also noted that Christ's ethic demanded both concern and action in the social arena. "If the principles of the Christian religion are not carried into *society*," he said, "if they are not carried into *business*, if they are not carried into *politics*, if we do not let the light shine; then the salt has lost the savor and the light is put under a bushel."[29]

Baptist seminarians like Carroll, Gardner, and Broadus were not the only Baptists who displayed social concern between 1890 and 1920. Denominational leaders such as Isaac Taylor Tichenor were also concerned with providing relief to the needy. Tichenor was born November 11, 1825, in Spencer County, Kentucky. When he was fifteen, he entered Taylorsville Academy but was stricken with measles before he could finish his education at the academy. Upon his recovery he taught briefly and even served Taylorsville Academy as principal for one year.[30]

While he was polishing his teaching skills, Tichenor also honed his oratorical talents in various Baptist pulpits. He was ordained in 1848 in Columbus, Mississippi, where he pastored until 1850. Tichenor went from Mississippi to Henderson, Kentucky, where he stayed for about one year. He then served as pastor of First Baptist Church in Montgomery, Alabama, for some fifteen years. During the Civil War, Tichenor served as chaplain of the 17th Alabama Regiment, where he saw action at Shiloh. After the Civil War, Tichenor astutely noted that Alabama possessed great natural mineral wealth, and he even predicted a coming day when Alabama's natural resources would lead the state to economic greatness. In 1871, Tichenor became president of Alabama's Agricultural and Mechanical College in Auburn, Alabama. He served in this capacity for more than ten years, and in June 1882, Tichenor resigned this position to become Corresponding Secretary of the Home Mission Board, a post he held until July 1899. He died in 1902.[31]

Throughout his life Tichenor exhibited a concern for social issues. As a minister he was also concerned that his church members would manifest an interest in the social conditions around them. According to his diary he preached a sermon in November 1850 titled "Claims of the Bible Upon the Consideration of All Men." It was a three-point sermon based on Matthew 11:15, "He that hath ears to hear, let him hear." Tichenor considered humankind as social, intellectual, and immortal beings. He said that as a social being man is "bound to his fellow man by the strongest ties and most unyielding interests." Consequently, everyone had a stake in the "welfare of the community in which he lives. All the interests of society are in some measure his interests." If people contributed to society negatively (i.e., by corrupting morals), they hurt others. Conversely, by exerting positive influence, it benefited all. As Tichenor put it, " . . . so entwined is this connection between the members of society that the injury of one is the injury of all and the improvement of one is the improvement of all."[32]

Tichenor further argued that religion was a powerful social force that influenced people in numerous ways that were frequently unknown by the religious population at large. The results, however, had been a blessing to society. "The principles of our holy religion," he said, "have in the past diffused themselves throughout the land, modifying the evils of society, lessening its abuses, diminishing the ills of all mankind."[33]

Tichenor closed this sermon by arguing that religion's greatest aim was neither social reformation nor advancing intellectual pursuits. Religion's greatest object was the betterment of humanity's spiritual condition. That is to say, the gospel's greatest claims were eternal, not temporal.[34] Nevertheless, Tichenor's reasoning is clear. If religion produced a spiritual change within an individual, that change would be translated into concern for the condition of others. Thus, social redemption had to be preceded by individual redemption. And for individuals to become "better," they needed to be converted to Christianity.

There is some evidence that Tichenor, an ambitious minister, was suspicious that those in the Christian world, himself included, were not as committed to God's cause in this world as they should be. On

November 11, 1850, he wrote, "This is my birthday—I am now twenty-five. Half the life I may reasonably expect to live is already gone, and yet how little have I done for God. Nearly four years since I entered the ministry and how little I have accomplished."[35] He then prayed that the Lord would help him to be more diligent in his twenty-sixth year.

Tichenor also feared that his preaching was inadequate. For example, after finally completing a Thanksgiving sermon, a diary notation of November 27, 1850, disclosed his dissatisfaction. It was a "poor thing," he said, and he was "almost ashamed" even to preach it.[36] He felt better about it one week later, on December 1, when he noted that his congregation was "deeply attentive" and many expressed interest in holding a revival meeting. Again, one week later he lapsed back into his melancholy. He had been working on a sermon titled, "The Nature, Extent and Influence of the Love of God." On December 6, he complained that he had done more daydreaming than contemplation. He plaintively said, "Would that my own heart were more deeply impressed with the greatness of this love and the obligations we are laid under by it, to live to God and not to ourselves."[37]

Clearly, Tichenor had high standards by which he judged his personal piety. He also had high standards for his congregation, especially regarding church business meetings. On one occasion he noted that "many of the brethren [are] careless about church meetings. This is a point upon which I shall at some time stir up their minds."[38]

This "stirring up" may have come in two separate messages. In a message on Hebrews 12:1–2 that is simply labeled "Revised in Henderson, December 1850," Tichenor said that everyone, including he himself, had been indolent in Christ's cause. He chided his congregation by noting that if everyone were as diligent in seeking the spiritual well-being of others as they were in gaining material wealth, the world would have more Christians. He also accused most Christians of "slumbering," oblivious to the world around them. He challenged his congregation to use its influence for good in the community in order that "the kingdoms of this world would become the Kingdoms of our Lord and his Christ."[39]

In a separate message titled "Religious Progress" he prepared for February 1, 1851, Tichenor likened contemporary Christians to the ancient Hebrews who were going into the Promised Land. He noted that once they had acquired part of Canaan, the Hebrews were content with what they already had. There was, however, much more to do. The same was true for Christians. They were not to be satisfied merely with their spiritual possessions; they must press onward. He noted, "We have all heard and all felt that the path of duty is the path of happiness. Tis only when we are thus diligent that we go from strength to strength."[40]

Tichenor's sermons, along with his brief diary entries, indicate that he wanted his congregation vitally involved in community affairs. His understanding of Christianity's social implications would not allow him to see his ministry or his congregation's activities any other way.

Perhaps Tichenor's broader social and economic concerns are clearer in his reports to the Board of Directors while he was President of Alabama's Agricultural and Mechanical College. He assumed this post in 1871, and for ten years he tried to build the institution's facilities, faculty, and enrollment. His reports reveal that Tichenor envisioned a New South built on social and economic advancement.

Early in his tenure at what would become Auburn University, Tichenor demonstrated his progressive thinking. In his second report to the board of directors he noted strong opposition from some to "book farming." Undaunted, he advised the board that Alabama was suffering from a lack of information regarding the best way to cultivate the state's soil. He then proposed that one man from each Alabama county be offered a scholarship to the college. The recipients would have to agree to become agriculturalists and stay at the college for the full course, and in return they would receive full tuition, board, books, and a uniform for one year at the rate of $100.[41]

Tichenor also demonstrated that his vision of a New South was not limited merely to an economy based on more sophisticated agriculture. Postwar economic woes, particularly the Panic of 1873, had hit the fledgling institution at Auburn quite hard. Tichenor knew he had an uphill battle on his hands, and the main problem was money. He had to compete for limited resources with other established institutions, particularly the University of Alabama. Despite this David-and-Goliath scenario, Tichenor rose to the challenge by emphasizing his college's unique potential to prepare young men for a new economic order. Speaking of the institution's main purpose, Tichenor said, "Its leading object is to teach those sciences related to Agriculture and Me-

Isaac T. Tichenor, Secretary of the Home Mission Board, 1882–1898.
(Courtesy of the Southern Baptist Historical Library and Archives,
Historical Commission, SBC, Nashville, Tennessee.)

chanical Arts. It fits young men to lead in all those enterprises designed to *develop the industrial interests of her country.* This is the education demanded by the wants of her country and in it are to be found the forces which are to mold the new civilizations of the South."[42] He further noted that Americans needed to be economically self-sufficient, and he saw young Auburn in the vanguard of this change. Speaking of the South, Alabama in particular, he said,

> Men must learn how to recuperate our wasted lands, how to increase the productive power of our labor, how to make our languishing agriculture profitable, how to construct and control machinery, how to utilize our immense resources of iron and coal before we can hope for any great or permanent improvement in the condition of our people.[43]

His efforts evidently paid dividends. In 1878, his annual report indicated an enrollment of 238 students, putting Auburn's college first among Alabama's state institutions.[44]

Tichenor's enthusiasm and vision were not confined to his board of directors. In a report to the governor, dated October 10, 1876, Tichenor reminded the governor that his was the only institution in the state dedicated to providing an education for the state's agricultural and mechanical classes. He pictured a state rich in mineral wealth, not to mention innumerable streams and rivers potentially powering various types of machinery. He then challenged the governor to help Auburn as the state had helped the University of Alabama.[45]

Toward the end of his tenure at Auburn, President Tichenor outlined a broadbased system of education wherein the various state institutions worked together. He saw education as perhaps the most important key to southern economic development. He said, "The New South is rapidly coming forward." He believed southerners, especially Alabamians, needed to adjust their thinking regarding education if they were to meet the challenges ahead.[46] There is no evidence to suggest that Tichenor had backed away from his earlier Christian idealism. He saw no conflict between the New South economy and his sense of Christian mission.

If these reports indicate that Tichenor eagerly anticipated a New South, they also reveal his love for the Old South. Prior to the Civil War, Tichenor had owned slaves and had risked his life at Shiloh. He nevertheless accepted southern defeat and urged others to learn from the lessons of Appomattox. He maintained that the South did not lose the war for lack of bravery or military leadership. Rather, Tichenor said that the Confederacy was based on an old economic order that had downplayed the importance of industrialization. He said, "They never comprehended that steam engines and railroads, that looms and shuttles, that plows and hoes and reapers constituted a prime element of a nation's strength upon the field of battle."[47] If Tichenor had his way, the New South would see the economic benefits of industrialization.

There is evidence that Tichenor did not accept defeat graciously. In fact, he harbored considerable bitterness as late as 1877, and in the early 1890s he was a leading advocate for a distinct agency that would produce Sunday school literature for Southern Baptists. In his sixth report to the board of directors he described the postwar South as a place where property had been lost, society thrown into chaos, and labor demoralized. Evoking Milton's image of Satan and his host being expelled from heaven, Tichenor observed that the erstwhile angels at least had someone to console them—even if it was Lucifer. The South, however, had no one. "A feeble effort was made to secure a rehabilitation of our state as to its political rights," he lamented, "but its paralyzed industry received no attention at their hands."[48]

In 1882, Tichenor left Auburn to become Secretary of the Home Mission Board. As his diary, sermons, and annual reports to Auburn's board of directors indicate, Tichenor was a man who expected great things from himself and others. He was something of a visionary, perhaps ahead of his time regarding economic philosophy. He was also an ardent southerner who retained a strong regional pride until his death. Finally, he was also concerned with the social conditions of those around him. In a memorial tribute to Tichenor, Lansing Burrows, recording secretary of the Southern Baptist Convention, praised Tichenor's passion for the South and the Baptist cause. He left the presidency of Auburn's college, Burrows said, because of his, *"passionate love for the South, his faith in its marvelous future, and his persuasion that, if his leadership should be followed, his people would attain to magnificent things for Christ and His cause."*[49]

Moreover, he dedicated the same energy and tenacity to his position as Secretary of the Home Mission Board that he had to his pastorates and the presidency at Auburn's Agricultural and Mechanical College. In 1885, he challenged the Southern Baptist Convention to visualize the good its united energies could accomplish. He challenged his fellow Southern Baptists to work harder and expect greater things. Evoking a military metaphor that doubtless stirred most of the convention's delegates, he said, "We are weary of following every other Christian host into the battle for the world's deliverance. We want to move up to the front, and as good soldiers bear our full part in the conflict."[50] This conflict was both spiritual and temporal. Tichenor envisioned a New Religious South, as well as a New Economic South. It would have greater opportunities than the Old South, but economic development had its price. The South needed to industrialize, and Tichenor understood that industrialization would create both economic and social changes. Such changes would require Southern Baptists to rethink their commitment to reaching people. One writer said of Tichenor, "He penetrated the possibilities of the then unknown mountain ranges, knowing the capabilities of their people, prophesying the development of their vast mineral accumulations and impressed by the value of their relations to the new conditions of the South."[51] Another writer noted that Tichenor wanted Southern Baptists to start schools; build hospitals, orphanages, and homes for the aged; and participate in those measures that would relieve people from the suffering they endured from sin.[52] In the 1890s he began to see his dream bear fruit.

Another leading spokesman for New South thinking in southern churches was not a cleric. He was Richard H. Edmunds, editor of *The Manufacturer's Record*. Edmunds is famous for his New South boosterism, and Paul M. Gaston describes him as the "longest lived of all the New South prophets."[53] While Gaston did not comment on Edmunds's faith, the fact that he was a Baptist was not lost on the Convention's leadership.

In 1910, the Southern Baptist Convention met in Baltimore, Maryland, Edmunds's home. He was honored to give the welcoming address. Reflecting both missionary zeal and economic boosterism, he informed his brethren that urbanization was the most pressing problem they faced, for urban restlessness and the cities' changing complexion undermined traditional religious folkways. Immigrants also posed a challenge because they did not know, " . . . our language, our laws, our civilization, our Christianity."[54] Yet all was not lost. If cities were problems, they were also opportunities. The key was evangelism.

Edmunds said, "Save the city for Christ, and you save the country. Save this country, and you save the world."[55]

Of course, Edmunds believed that Baptists were poised to do just that. They had the resources to fund great evangelistic undertakings. The real issue was whether Baptists would be "faithful stewards." That is, given their resources, both cultural and human, Edmunds wondered if Baptists would rise to the challenge. He believed that the South was rapidly urbanizing, and he warned that many contemporary villages would blossom into towns and that many towns would become centers of economic life. Thus, Baptists needed to be on their guard. "As Baptists," Edmunds warned, "we must keep step with population or towns and cities will be lost forever to our cause."[56]

Edmunds's attitude, like Tichenor's, reflected the idea that hard work and faithfulness would solve numerous social and economic problems. Baptists could cite numerous scripture references to make this point. After all, had not Paul admonished the Corinthians that God required Christians to be faithful stewards?[57] According to Tichenor and Edmunds, stewardship also encouraged Baptists to support denominational causes, particularly missions, with open wallets. As one wealthy Baptist noted, "We must wake up our rich Baptists. If they do not turn their money loose for God and His cause it will ruin them. . . . A man that has money and is making money, needs to pray a great deal, and keep close to God, in order to save himself from trouble."[58]

Few Baptists disagreed with Edmunds's and Tichenor's visionary spirit. Most believed that the South had entered a new era of prosperity. They also believed they were responsible for the wise usage of their resources and talents. Moreover, many leading Southern Baptists displayed a genuine concern for society's dispossessed.

There is no denying the Baptist evangelical impulse. The primary concern was to save individuals from damnation, but this precluded neither social concern nor social action. The nexus upon which conversion and activism hinged was the idea that better people made a better society. Baptists believed that conversion should foster fundamental changes precipitated by repentance within individuals. Hence, as more people became Christians and applied their new ethic to society's problems, they should create a better society.[59]

Clearly, ameliorating social problems was first a matter of getting one's soul right with God. Victor Masters, Superintendent of Publicity for the Home Mission Board, articulated this basic assumption clearly in 1912 when he observed that society was characterized by "social unrest," the root problem of which was ethics. He admonished churches not to fear social unrest because Christianity was responsible. "The social unrest of today," he said, "is because Christianity in the hearts and minds of the people has created higher standards of living, correcter [sic] ideas of human brotherhood, and a deeper conviction that justice must rule in society."[60] He then asked rhetorically if Christianity should lead the legal fight for social betterment. Although Masters offered no unequivocal answer, he did propose a guiding principle. He said, "The personal and spiritual are always of more moment than the political and social."[61] This is another way of saying that better people create better societies. Masters concluded his discourse by arguing that Christianity had been a world leader in the quest for social justice. He further noted that "if the churches shall fail to do their duty for social betterment today, it will be because they have failed at the task of making better men rather than because of failure from their declining to become for the public the leaders of social adjustment and the teachers of social science."[62]

Richard Edmunds later responded favorably to Masters's article and even added his own reflections. Churches were obligated to preach the gospel and oversee the religious development of their membership. True, some social topics were worthwhile. Nevertheless, he believed that churches needed to be involved in making Christians. Otherwise, he warned, churches whose ministers dwelt on the "subjects" and "isms" of the day were likely to lose influence in the community.[63]

Separating economic boosterism from missionary impulse, or from general optimism in the South's immediate future, was no easy matter. Southern Baptist denominational leadership was fiercely loyal to the region, and with Baptist educational institutions training future leaders, they anticipated a bright future. Moreover, with men like Edmunds touting the southern economy, the future appeared even brighter.

Still, there were concerns, and these leaders did not hesitate to voice them. With prosperity at the door, many feared that southerners would become consumed in greed and bow before the god of mammon. Some saw urbanization on the South's horizon and along with it the problems of large cities. Still others wondered what increased immigration would mean for the South. The problem was that unconverted people could not be left to themselves, especially during dramatic social change.

Here again, evangelism met social concern. Southern Baptist leaders believed that preaching was the answer for each of these issues. They believed that if church members learned Christian stewardship, money would not become a problem. They were prepared to tackle urban problems by preaching. If they were correct in believing better people made better societies, it would be true for all social strata. Finally, they believed that immigrants, many of whom were Jewish or Catholic, needed the gospel. Hence, they saw the church as being equipped to handle all potential social issues.

Translating social concern into Social Christianity then became a matter of missionary activity. In some areas Baptists could rely on Biblical mandates to become involved in social action, while in other areas they could not. In either case, their views and activities were always framed by their theological assumptions, particularly that of individual salvation.

4

SOUTHERN BAPTISTS, SOCIAL CHRISTIANITY, AND ORPHANAGES

"Suffer the little children to come unto Me, and forbid them not: for of such is the Kingdom of God."

Mark 10:14

Southern baptist benevolence was particularly pronounced between 1890 and 1920, but it was not confined exclusively to that era. This was especially true regarding Baptist commitment to caring for orphaned children. Understanding how Southern Baptists ministered to the needy, especially orphans, is a compelling aspect of Social Christianity in the South because it clearly demonstrates the method and ideological assumptions Baptists employed to address societal ills.

Southern Baptists organized several orphanages prior to 1890, most of which originally ministered to Civil War orphans. The Mississippi Baptists discussed their need for such a facility as early as 1864. Initially, this venture was not limited strictly to the Baptist denomination, but when the Baptists met with representatives from other Protestant denominations in the state, they were unable to devise a plan whereby no single denomination would exert dominant influence. Consequently, the Baptists decided to establish their own institution in Lauderdale, Mississippi.[1]

Unfortunately, this institution was doomed to fail due largely to the fact that it had to accommodate too many children. The orphanage officially opened in October 1866, with two girls, but by May 1867, there were 106 resident orphans, and by 1868, this number had ballooned to over 230.[2]

It would have been difficult to care for these children under optimal conditions, but the Civil War had destroyed Mississippi's economy and the orphanage languished for lack of finances. W. S. Webb, secretary of the Home's Board, was particularly distressed by the circumstances. He estimated that there were some 5,000 to 10,000 orphans in the state and some 50,000 Baptists whom he chided for neglecting Biblical commands to care for the poor and needy. Webb then challenged his brethren and fellow Mississippians to raise twenty-five cents for each of the state's 100,000 men and women. This, he noted, would provide an annual budget of at least $25,000. Failure to maintain the institution, he warned, "would mark us with a pusillanimity that would deserve the contempt of the world."[3] Besides, Webb added, this institution was the only one of its kind in the state not under Catholic control.[4]

This challenge went unheeded, but it may not have been because Mississippians were tightfisted. One of the Home's main problems was that its board of trustees was not composed entirely of Baptists. The ecumenical board of trustees bickered over who would control the orphanage. The result was internal factionalism between those who favored less denominational control of the facility and the Baptists in Mississippi who wanted more control. This situation led Webb to lament, "The Board is placed under very embarrassing circumstances; They can turn neither to the right hand nor to the left; on the one hand Scylla, on the other Charybdis; in front the boisterous sea, behind the wailing cry of a helpless orphanage; the current running across our course, and threatening to engulf us."[5] Engulf them it did. By the mid-1870s the orphanage was disbanded.

Much like its Mississippi counterpart, the Louisville Baptist Orphans Home dates back to the immediate post–Civil War era. As early as 1866, Dr. George C. Lorimer, pastor of the Walnut Street Baptist Church in Louisville, Kentucky, expressed deep concern for children whose parents had died in the Civil War. Lorimer was also concerned about other children who might not be war orphans, but were nevertheless destitute owing to the war or other circumstances.[6]

While Lorimer's motives were indeed noble, they were not entirely altruistic. According to Grace Lewis Hardaway, Lorimer had already been forced to recommend that several Baptist children go to the local Catholic orphanage, recognizing that there were no Baptist agencies to accommodate orphans. One day he learned that the Catholic sisters from the local orphanage had been soliciting funds from a fellow minister to help maintain their institution since a good number of their children had come from Baptist households. The sisters reminded this minister that it was not unreasonable to expect that Baptists should help raise their own children.[7]

This was too much! Lorimer called the Ladies Aid Society of his church together. This Society was an auxiliary of the Walnut Street Baptist Church and gave women an opportunity to do benevolent work under the auspices of their church. In fact, some of these women were already actively helping orphans by paying their rent in local boarding houses or trying to find them permanent homes. The women agreed with their pastor that more could be done for the local orphans, and in 1866, they formed the Orphans Aid Society. Ultimately, this group planned to build a fully functional orphanage.[8]

A similar concern for Civil War orphans motivated the North Carolina Baptists. Rather than beginning a denominational institution, however, Baptists in the Tar Heel State were content to support a Masonic orphanage until 1884, when John Haymes Mills resigned as the home's superintendent. Prior to 1884, Mills had managed the home almost single-handedly, but the Grand Lodge believed the job was too much for one individual. Thus, they gave the authority for running the home to a six-member board of directors.[9]

Immediately upon Mills's resignation *The Biblical Recorder*, a Baptist newspaper in North Carolina, began receiving letters calling for a new orphanage. One letter signed "Warrenton" maintained that Christians had a duty to exhibit their faith by their deeds. Moreover, since many were already giving money to support "human institutions," it was time for Baptists to assume the responsibility of maintaining their own institution. That is, "Warrenton" advocated an institution not merely for Baptist orphans, but one "supported and managed by Baptists for the benefit of all orphans who come and comply with the rules of admission."[10] Two weeks later *The Biblical Recorder* received a letter from the Reverend Columbus Durham, a North Carolina Baptist minister. He found several good reasons to establish a new orphanage. In addition to having a God-given responsibility to care for orphaned children, Durham argued that it would be better to have an institution supported by freewill offerings than one maintained by state appropriations. Moreover, he maintained that the state's Baptist churches could support such an institution without conflicting with similar institutions. Besides, a new denominational orphanage would provide Baptist women with an opportunity to minister in the home as matrons. He concluded his letter by suggesting that J. H. Mills, W. R. Gwaltney, and R. D. Fleming comprise a committee to investigate the possibility of building an orphanage. This committee, Durham suggested, should be prepared to report its findings at the next state Convention.[11]

When the North Carolina Baptists met in Convention in the fall of 1884, one of the more pressing issues was whether or not North Carolina Baptists should establish an orphanage. What ensued was a bitter debate that left the Convention badly divided. Many Baptists, particularly the Rev. A. G. McManaway, pastor of First Baptist Church in Louisburg, North Carolina, argued that the Masons already had a facility in Oxford through which the Baptists could funnel their benevolence. Consequently, they believed a Baptist orphanage was unnecessary. Besides, he estimated that it would cost $25,000 to fund a new institution.[12]

When the Convention adjourned without taking action on the orphanage, John C. Scarborough, W. R. Gwaltney, George W. Greene, R. R. Overby, E. Frost, Dr. Charles E. Taylor, J. D. Hufham, and Columbus Durham organized the North Carolina Baptist Orphanage Association on November 15, 1884. Mills was the unanimous choice to be the Home's first General Manager.[13]

In spite of the initial opposition, the Mills Home, as it came to be known, became a permanent feature of Baptist life in North Carolina. In fact, on November 11, 1885, the fledgling orphanage received its first child—less than one year after the state convention failed to agree to take any action. Even Rev. A. G. McManaway, initially an opponent of the orphanage, became a member of the Orphanage Association and served as its recording secretary.[14]

Unlike their brethren in other states, the Texas Baptists were not driven primarily by compassion for Civil War orphans. Nor was the first Baptist orphanage in Texas established in response to perceived Roman Catholic threats or to personality conflicts within local Masonic lodges. Texans got their first taste of caring for orphans thanks to Robert Cooke Buckner.

Buckner was a Baptist minister who came to Texas in 1859, after successful pastorates in Kentucky. On January 3, 1874, he became the editor of *The Religious Messenger*, a small denominational newspaper in north Texas. One year later Buckner moved the paper to Dallas, whereupon it became known as *The Texas Baptist*. Buckner used this medium to communicate his dream of establishing a Baptist orphanage in Texas. He called for the deacons in Texas Baptist churches to meet in Paris, Texas, in July 1877. Citing such passages as James 1:27 and Acts 6:1–6, he reminded them that deacons had a God-given duty to care for widows and orphans. Approximately one hundred deacons present at this meeting agreed with Buckner and passed a resolution to establish a home for orphaned children. Buckner also became the home's first general superintendent, a position he held until his death in 1919.[15]

By comparing the homes in Mississippi, Kentucky, North Carolina, and Texas, it is clear that these facilities followed no prescribed pattern for organization and development. Neither did these facilities serve as models for subsequent orphanages. No other subsequent Southern Baptist orphanage addressed orphanhood from an ecumenical perspective. No other institution summoned the talents of the state's deacons the way Buckner did in Texas. The Louisville Baptist Orphans Home was sponsored and maintained by the churches in the Long Run Association and *not* by the state convention, a fact that made this home unique. Of the four, the North Carolina home perhaps came closest to setting a pattern for later homes, and even at that, no other Baptist home had ties to the Masons like those of the Mills Home.

Dissimilarities aside, these homes all shared important features. In each case, the Baptists within the state identified orphanhood as a distinct social problem. With state governments unable to provide relief for orphans, Baptists demonstrated a remarkable willingness to assume the burden. Additionally, the Baptists in each of these states believed that Christians, or more specifically, churches had a divine mandate to care for orphans. Their origins varied from state to state, but the basic motivation to start a Baptist orphanage was always the same. On the one hand, God required them to have compassion for orphans; on the other hand, the orphan's cry was so pitiful that they simply could not turn away and pretend no problems existed. Thus, each of these institutions represent the merger of social concern with religious action.

In 1890, Southern Baptists boasted five orphanages. By the end of the decade, they operated eleven. By 1920, each southern state had its own Baptist orphanage, and some states, such as North Carolina and Kentucky, had two homes. In fact, some states that opened orphanages after the Civil War only to see them closed owing to financial difficulties, reopened orphanages after 1890.[16]

Since these institutions were financed primarily through private contributions, what triggered this rapid increase in Baptist benevolence? The answers are varied. An improving southern economy may have put more money into Baptist church members' hands. This, in turn, may have contributed to the increased number of orphanages between 1890 and 1920.

Another factor that may have contributed to this increase in benevolence lies within the Baptists themselves. Some Southern Baptist historians have suggested that the turn of the century was a pivotal time in Baptist history because it demonstrated a keen and intensifying self-awareness among Southern Baptists. Rapid population increases tantalized Baptists with prospects of new members. Technological innovations like the typewriter and linotype improved journalism and refined one of the more potent weapons in the Baptist arsenal, the printed word. The influence these factors exerted is reflected in such institutional undertakings as the Home Mission Board and the Sunday School Board.[17]

Because so much Southern Baptist thought and action is geared toward evangelism, one might assume that if Baptists became increasingly self-conscious between 1890 and 1920, this "awareness" would manifest itself primarily in evangelistic fervor. But the institutions they built also reflect this increasing denominational self-awareness among Southern Baptists. Stated simply, Baptists were beginning to see their mission in terms of both evangelization *and* social outreach to the less fortunate.

Since Baptists saw caring for homeless children as a type of missionary activity, orphanages depended on individual benevolence for their financial survival. This method was not always reliable in the immediate post–Civil War years where Baptists in Mississippi and Georgia tried unsuccessfully to build homes for orphans. Such, however, was not always the case, and those orphanages established after 1890 have survived until the present. In fact, those orphanages that

Southern Baptist Orphanages were cooperative ventures. Here a group from the Mississippi Children's Home is receiving goods collected from churches throughout the state. (Courtesy of The Baptist Children's Village, Jackson, Mississippi.)

failed in the 1860s and 1870s enjoyed a renaissance in the 1890s. While it is true that these institutions frequently faced scarcity, they somehow found a way to survive.

The significant aspect about financing these institutions is the ingenious ways southerners employed to fund such ventures. Of course, the most obvious way to raise money was through direct appeal. Once organized, orphanages usually gave reports when the churches met in State Convention. Here, messengers heard about the institution's needs and learned of the previous year's successes or failures. It was then up to the messengers to report back to the churches. For example, when the Georgia Baptist Convention met in 1900, the orphanage report stated: "We have at present sixty-five children in our keeping. Shall we close our doors upon other friendless little ones, for want of help from our Christian friends?"[18] Once the institutions published their needs, churches responded in a variety of ways. Some sent monthly support to the institutions. Others received special offerings during the year, especially at Thanksgiving and Christmas. Some churches did both.

Another method by which orphanages could solicit support was to request that churches assist one child. In South Carolina the Board of Managers at the Connie Maxwell Home calculated the cost of maintaining one child to be about six dollars a month. This figure included everything the child needed, but did not include the cost of maintaining buildings. Representatives of the home could then present this figure to interested persons or churches and encourage them to support one or more children rather than making a more broadly based appeal for the institution. Moreover, this figure was so reasonable that some Sunday school classes could support a child in the orphanage as a special project. Apparently, this was an extremely effective way to solicit support. According to A. T. Jamison, an early superintendent of South Carolina's Connie Maxwell Home, eight of the home's twenty-six children were supported this way in the facility's first year of operation.[19]

Such appeals were not confined to monetary matters. In 1898 and 1899, the Louise Short Widows and Orphans Home appealed to those assembled at the State Convention for a "sick ward." This orphanage had access to a doctor, but they believed a sick ward would greatly enhance their facility.[20] It was not uncommon for Baptist orphanages to receive gifts ranging from barrels of flour and sugar to boxes of clothing and toys. Livestock was also a common gift, especially to rural orphanages. In one of the more amusing incidents, R. C. Buckner wrote a thank-you note to a certain Mrs. Dinwiddie that read:

Dear Mrs. Dinwiddie:
    The basket of eggs were received in good order and are under a fine large hen. You have our sincere thanks and best wishes.

> Very Cordially,
> R. C. Buckner[21]

As insignificant as such a donation may appear to contemporary readers, the homes greatly appreciated whatever gifts they received. As Buckner's note implies, if handled correctly, a basket of eggs could be converted into a flock of chickens. Helping orphanages, then, was an enterprise that assumed a variety of forms and could be tackled by everyone as a missionary enterprise.

If state conventions provided an opportunity for orphanages to discuss their needs, they also provided a forum to chide fellow Baptists for not doing more to assist the state's needy. W. C. Golden, president of the Board of Managers of the Tennessee Baptist Orphans Home, scolded the state's churches in 1896 for not being more generous. Golden said, "Just why some of these do not furnish a road into all our hearts for this institution it is hard to tell. It would seem that *sympathy* for the orphans should move us; and if not sympathy, *compassion*; and if not compassion, the love for Him Who loved the orphan, or loyalty to His biddings, or pride in the success of denomination undertaking, or *something* ought to stir us to a more concerted action for this work that is the very heart of religion, and is so very near the heart of God."[22]

Golden's pointed appeal cuts to the heart of what motivated concern for orphaned children. Baptists in the South did have sympathy and compassion for homeless children. Likewise, they sincerely believed that caring for orphaned children was a heavenly mandate, and they wanted to fulfill God's will in this area. Nevertheless, Golden also identified an issue that was becoming increasingly important: denominational pride. In addition to expressing their personal compassion and fulfilling scriptural mandates, Baptists were increasingly expecting their benevolent institutions to reflect their social awareness. In 1910, the Georgia Baptists lamented the fact that Baptists left numerous benevolent enterprises, such as caring for the poor and destitute, to "fraternal organizations" like the Masons. Consequently, these "fraternal organizations" received credit and worldly recognition for performing social duties that rightfully belonged to churches. This sentiment clearly was not confined to Georgia because the Arkansas Baptists voiced similar concerns in 1918. Certain Baptists reasoned that if 21,000 or 22,000 Masons could build an orphanage, the state's 125,000 Baptists could surely do likewise.

Golden's appeal also reflects the frustration that all orphanage administrators experienced regarding finances. While it is true that Baptists gave sacrificially, it is also true that the orphanages encountered more financial stress as they expanded their ministries. Indeed, the cost of even starting an orphanage was enough to make the most farsighted visionary think twice. Institutions needed physical plants, staff personnel, and supplies. Here again, however, Baptists, and in some cases even non-Baptists, proved equal to the task.

The Connie Maxwell Home in South Carolina illustrates this point well. Here, Baptists began discussing the need for an orphanage as early as 1888, but they could not agree upon a site for the Home until 1891. This was because the committee originally appointed to look into the matter had numerous offers to consider. These offers came from twelve different areas and included cash, or real estate, or both. The committee finally settled upon the offer made by the city of Greenwood, South Carolina, and some of its citizens, including Dr. and Mrs. J. C. Maxwell. The offer amounted to about $35,000, most of which Dr. Maxwell single-handedly provided. The town of Greenwood pledged ten acres of land and the citizens pledged $2,200. Maxwell proposed to grant a mortuary deed on 470 acres of land just outside of town, plus ten acres of land in Greenwood. In order for the Baptists to receive this gift, Maxwell stipulated that the orphanage be built at or near Greenwood and that it be named in honor of Constance "Connie" Maxwell, the doctor's deceased daughter. The doctor's generosity and sincerity notwithstanding, he apparently had some reservations. He wryly noted that "if the Baptists do not keep up said Orphanage in a more businesslike and liberal manner than they sustain their pastors, churches, and Universities, the will would probably be revoked."[23] These reservations aside, the Connie Maxwell Home became one of the most successful of all Southern Baptist orphanages.

A final method that Southern Baptists used to finance their orphanages was through individual Home endowments. There was no consensus on this point, and Baptists tended to polarize their opinions around two extremes. Some Baptists favored endowments; others did not. The latter believed that endowments constituted a lack of faith in God's ability to provide through freewill offerings. Moreover, some maintained that rank-and-file church members had less motivation to give sacrificially to a home with an endowment than to one without an endowment. It was, quite simply, very difficult to convince people that an institution needed funds when it had money in the bank.

The homes in Texas and Kentucky represent the extremes regarding this issue. In 1906, R. C. Buckner pointed out that the Buckner Orphans Home had considerable real estate holdings but no endowment. Interestingly, that same report noted that the previous year's receipts totaled $64,552.54, while the debts totaled $60,846.54. At the same time there were over 600 children living at the Home. Clearly, Buckner believed his facility needed no endowment.[24]

On the other hand, in 1914, the Louisville Baptist Orphans Home reported a total endowment of $303,640, while the home's total enrollment was over 100. The Finance Committee report for 1914 indicates that the endowment consisted of real estate holdings in Louisville and east Texas, as well as stocks, bonds, and cash. A considerable portion of these assets came from a certain Captain William F. Norton's estate. In 1891, Norton gave the home $5,000 on behalf of him and his mother, provided that the Kentucky Baptists could raise an additional $22,000 for an addition to the orphanage. A 1903 report to the General Association of Baptists (Kentucky Baptist Convention) indicates that Norton had died and bequeathed a "substantial amount" to the Home.[25]

Of course, most homes needed whatever donations they could garner for day-to-day operation. Yet gifts to Baptist orphanages did not always come in small amounts from poorer donors. Some homes had wealthy benefactors who supported the institutions liberally. Moreover, increased yearly offerings reflect a tendency for Baptist benevolence to cut across a broad spectrum of socioeconomic classes. Overall, Baptist concern for the needy, as evidenced by support for denominational orphanages, increased dramatically between 1890 and 1920.

For example, in South Carolina the Connie Maxwell Home reported a total income of $11,261.88 in 1892. The same institution reported a total income of $23,478.88 for 1903. Although $8,250 of this sum came from the sale of a portion of the Maxwell estate that had been left to the Home upon Dr. and Mrs. Maxwell's deaths, more than $15,000 came from individuals and churches in the state. By 1910, the Connie Maxwell Home reported total receipts of $34,208.45. This number had almost tripled to $91,606.96 in 1918, and by 1920, the home reported a total income of $161,778.58.[26] Other Southern Baptist orphanages boasted similar increases. Clearly, Baptists manifested their social concern with an increasing desire to commit their resources to helping needy children.

Committing financial resources to a project, however, only partially reflected Baptist concern for homeless children. By examining the facilities and what they had to offer, it is possible to see that Baptist benevolence was far more than simple charity designed to ameliorate suffering. In a traditional culture strongly rooted in values of place and family, orphanages were homes that provided stability and the hope of a future in a changing world.

In each case Baptist orphanages sought to provide a family atmosphere for the children they received. Traditionally Baptists placed great emphasis on the family as a God-ordained institution and, since the orphaned children had been deprived of their home and families, administrators sought to create a homelike atmosphere within the institution. Charles Linwood Corbitt, the first superintendent of the Virginia Baptist Orphans Home, was constantly planting flowers and working to beautify the institution. His motivation was simple: He wanted to make the children happy. The same was true in South Carolina, where A. T. Jamison insisted that time be set aside for children to play. He reasoned that children who had suffered the greatest human loss at least deserved to have as happy a childhood as the staff at Connie Maxwell could provide. In fact, the underlying philosophy at Connie Maxwell reflected the attitude of all Southern Baptist orphanages. They saw orphaned children not as societal castaways, but as children needing direction. Moreover, they believed that if children needed parenting before their parent's death, they likewise needed it afterward, and these institutions tried to provide it.[27]

One of the first issues Baptists faced in establishing orphanages was housing. Although physical facilities varied from one home to another, Southern Baptists generally housed orphans according to either one of two plans. The barracks or dormitory plan is self-explanatory; children lived in a barrackslike facility. The obvious advantage to a barracks plan was economy, as it required a minimum number of buildings to get the orphanage started. The "cottage plan," however, was more elaborate. In the "cottage plan" each cottage served as a self-sustaining unit complete with a housemother. Each cottage also functioned according to its own schedule, which was determined independently from the other cottages. This was especially true of the Connie Maxwell Home where the administrators wanted to approximate as closely as possible a genuine home environment.[28]

Unfortunately, there was no consensus among Baptists regarding housing for orphans. This fact is reflected by Baptists in Maryland and the District of Columbia, who in the 1920s were planning to build a new orphanage. Incorporated in 1914, Maryland's Baptist Home for Children quickly outgrew its original Brookland, District of Columbia, location. In 1924, this home's board of trustees purchased a farm in nearby Montgomery County, Maryland, and began raising money to build their new facility. The challenge was to build the best possible facility for the children at the most reasonable cost, and they had a variety of options. They could build according to what they called the "congregate system" and have one central administration building with the children housed in one or two other buildings. The problem with this system, as they saw it, was that it destroyed individuality and labeled the children with the "orphanage stamp." The so-called cottage system was another option, but the Maryland Baptists knew this plan would require more than three buildings and be substantially more expensive than the congregate system. Their final option was the "placing out system," a forerunner of modern foster care. Under this plan the Maryland orphanage would house each orphan on a temporary basis until it found a private family willing to care for the child. The board of trustees finally settled on the "congregate system" when Edwin W. Gould, son of the notorious Robber Baron Jay Gould, donated $84,000 to build a girls' dormitory. Baptists in the District of Columbia raised the necessary funding for a boys' dorm.[29]

Regardless of the building plan, Baptist orphanages were vitally concerned with creating a homelike atmosphere, and this emphasis is reflected in a variety of ways. For example, when orphanages made reports to their respective state conventions, they usually included a brief census. It was not uncommon for reports to list the number of occupants as "family members." An early Buckner Orphans Home annual for 1891–1892 reports that the "family" consisted of 202. They came from diverse backgrounds and circumstances but functioned as nearly like a family as they could. "The children," wrote Buckner, "work as members of a family, play as members of a family, go to the table as members of a family, meet and sing and worship as a family, and are instructed to regard their interests as blended."[30] Buckner stressed, however, that each child was treated as an individual especially regarding property rights, temperament, tastes, capacities (abilities), and responsibilities.[31]

Ideally, most institutions wanted to find new homes for their orphaned children. This could be accomplished two ways. In Kentucky it was possible to adopt children through the home, provided, of course, that both the adopting parents and prospective adoptees agreed. The home also expected prospective parents to meet certain moral qualifications. For instance, one could never adopt a child for the purpose of making him or her a servant. Further, the home expected prospective parents to provide an adequate education for the children, including both religious education and public or private school.[32]

Another way of placing children involved apprenticeship. This required that children be taken from the home and taught a given trade. Here again, those apprenticing children were not allowed to make them into "servants," and they were expected to care for the child in ways not unlike natural parents.[33]

Apprenticing children was not a favored practice among Baptists. In fact, it was not even practical in most cases owing to the rural nature of most Baptist orphanages. Neither was adoption always a favored option in providing childcare. Many Baptists in the South expressed the same concerns that their Kentucky brethren did. R. C. Buckner had particularly strong opinions on this point. In 1907, he estimated that in his thirty years' experience, nineteen of twenty who wanted to adopt children had "selfish motives," which he described as the desire to adopt a child simply for the sake of having a child. He believed that such individuals did not have the child's best interests at heart. Buckner also noted that once children were adopted it was difficult for them to become part of a new family. If a couple already had children they tended to treat the adopted child differently from the natural children. On the other hand, if the adopting parents had no children, they scarcely knew how to make a home. Consequently, Buckner saw the orphanage as a viable, in most cases even preferable, alternative to adoption. Since it was not subject to such things as divorce, it was stable and offered the orphaned child a place to stay, as well as food and medical attention.[34]

The Tennessee Baptists went one step further. In 1911, they decided to keep their children as wards of the institution and not become what they deemed a "home-finding" agency. Contrary to Buckner's concerns, they believed that it was not possible to maintain a familylike atmosphere if the institution experienced constant arrivals and departures. They also believed they were doing a disservice to their children if they let them leave the home without some type of formal training.[35]

In addition to providing a homelike setting, Baptist orphanages in the South sought to provide children with an education. The Louisville Baptist Orphans Home operated a school where the children, male and female, studied spelling, arithmetic, geography, and English grammar. Students usually spent about five hours a day in school, and Mrs. E. V. Robertson, co-editor of *The Orphans' Friend*, was one of the first teachers.[36] And, as one might expect, Mrs. Robertson had her hands full when it came to teaching her streetwise students. On one particular day Mr. J. W. Rust, a school examiner who later became a representative of the home, stopped by for a visit. While there, he spoke to the nursery-aged children regarding the five senses. When he left, one disgruntled tyke reportedly said, "I hain't seen nothen of them nickels yet."[37]

In 1915, the children at the Louisville Home had begun to attend public schools. The rationale behind this policy change involved finances and the children's welfare. It was cheaper to send them to public schools. Moreover, it allowed for socialization with other children from outside the orphanage. Besides, the children still received tutoring at the Home after school.[38]

The Louisville facility's urban setting made it unique. Most Southern Baptist orphanages were rural and did not enjoy the advantages of an urban public school system. There are no explicit statements indicating that Baptists were overly suspicious of urban areas. The one that comes closest to this sentiment is in Bernard Washington Spilman's work on the Mills Home. He says simply, "Mr. Mills always held that the city was not the best location for an orphanage."[39] A. T. Jamison maintained that the country was more advantageous than the city for raising children. Nevertheless, he cautioned, "This does not mean that it [an orphanage] should be miles and miles from town."[40]

Placing children in rural areas may have been a matter of space. Urban land was too expensive to purchase if one wanted enough room for children to have playgrounds. There may even have been other, more practical, considerations. Homes in rural areas could help defray institutional expenses by raising some of their own food. For instance,

Agriculture was a central feature of Baptist orphanages as this barn on
the grounds of the Mississippi Children's Home shows. (Courtesy of
The Baptist Children's Village, Jackson, Mississippi.)

each cottage at the Connie Maxwell Home had its own chicken house
and the Home maintained a dairy. In 1903, the Alabama Home reported that it had set out 800 peach trees, 500 plum, 110 pecan, plus
pear, quince, fig trees, and grapevines. The report also says that the
value of the Home's agricultural assets were about $175 for the year.[41]

The rural setting for the Homes did not prohibit residents from receiving an education. In fact, these rural Homes were vitally concerned with providing their charges with an academic background that
was as broad as their resources would permit. The Tennessee Home is
a good example. Originally, this institution was built close enough to
Nashville for the children to attend public schools. The 1909 report to
the State Convention proudly noted that all students "made the
grade." This same report indicated that by this time Nashville had
grown to the point that the facility was "crowded" by the city.[42] Thus,
the Home had been moved further into the country. One of the main
reasons for the move ironically involved a concern for industrial education. As the report argued, "in this age of the world we are doing a
boy a serious injustice when we send him out into the world without
some sort of careful industrial training."[43] A. T. Jamison agreed. He

maintained that both boys and girls "should be fitted to accept a job for themselves, having been trained practically, mechanically, commercially, or otherwise, to take their own real position in society."[44]

Georgia Baptists were a bit more explicit and innovative when it came to education. In 1902, the Home had 88 school-age children. In spite of having recently purchased 21 desks, the Home's school needed more equipment. "We hope," read the report to the state convention, "a Baptist Carnegie will rise up and equip this department for us."[45] Whether or not a "Baptist Carnegie" was forthcoming is unknown. At any rate, in 1911 the Home reported that its school had 153 students, three teachers, eight grades, and a curriculum similar to that of the Georgia public schools. This report also indicated that several students had gone to other unspecified institutions for further training and others were in nurse's training at Tabernacle Infirmary.[46] Even more encouraging were the reports for 1914 and 1920. By 1914, the Home was operating a telegraphy school and boasted thirteen graduates who had secured jobs in telegraph offices. Moreover, by 1920, the Home assisted truly talented students in their chosen vocations in spite of its school's limitations. T. S. Scroggins, manager of the Georgia Home said, "If facilities of our organization do not permit of a chosen training, Atlanta offers opportunities in any line. If one is sent to the city for vocational training they are paid a stipend, which enables them to be self-supporting."[47]

Other Home schools also boasted impressive programs. In North Carolina, the Mills Home's school curriculum included such things as reading, writing, Latin, algebra, composition, grammar, geography, occasionally Greek, and, of course, Bible, a subject that all orphanage schools taught. In Mississippi, where the mandatory school year was only six months in 1910, the orphanage proudly noted that its school had an eight-month calendar. Finally, in South Carolina the Connie Maxwell Home tried to keep abreast of changing needs in its school. Originally, there were seven grades, but the administration added an eighth grade in 1900, a tenth grade in 1905, and a twelfth grade later in the 1920s. By 1928, however, all high school children attended nearby Greenwood High School.[48]

Southern Baptist orphanages also tried to provide medical attention when the children were ill. From its earliest days the Louisville Baptist Orphans Home had an infirmary. This infirmary had its own bathroom with hot and cold running water. It also had five large windows overlooking hills, trees, and meadows. There were four beds and four chairs in the infirmary, and it was staffed by female residents. Miss Hollingsworth reported that, "A large girl and a small girl remain during the day with the sick, the large girl making poultices, applying warm flannels, preparing nourishment or administering medicine, assisted by the little girl. At night, they are relieved by two other girls."[49] Exactly what distinguished large and small girls is unclear. If age was the most important factor, a "large" girl was probably a teenager.

As unsophisticated as this practice may appear, it was successful. There were apparently a number of doctors, members of Louisville Baptist churches, who donated their attention to sick orphans. The 1910 Louisville Baptist Orphans Home report to the Kentucky Convention specifically mentioned Dr. J. B. Marvin as having rendered service to the Home's ill. Additionally, the report noted that as of 1910 the Home had admitted a total of 1,480 children. Of that number, only twenty-four had died. This is indeed a remarkably low number when one considers that the Home had no real control over the physical condition of the children they admitted. The report indicated that the Board of Managers believed this death-to-admission ratio may have been among the lowest in the world at that time.[50]

Not all institutions were as fortunate as the Louisville Baptist Orphans Home. Tight finances forced some facilities to relegate infirmaries to their "wish list." All facilities, however, understood the benefits of providing medical attention for their children. As noted earlier, the Alabama Baptists made a "sick room" a priority, because of the ever-present threat of epidemics. Other institutions doubtless had similar sentiments but most facilities, like the one in Louisville, enjoyed medical attention that was either donated by Baptist doctors or provided for a nominal cost. For example, in Mississippi the orphanage enjoyed the services of a certain Dr. Fulgham until he died in 1911. In 1914, Dr. G. L. Todd replaced Fulgham, and four nurses from the Jackson, Mississippi, churches likewise donated their time.[51]

Assessing the impact these institutions made and placing them within a broader social context is no easy matter. Superficially, it is tempting to consider Southern Baptist orphanages as a specialized, denominationally maintained version of American asylums. In *The Discovery of the Asylum*, David J. Rothman argues that antebellum asylums stemmed from an attempt to promote social stability at a time when society was changing rapidly and traditional modes of social control seemed ineffective. "The almshouse and the orphan asylum, the penitentiary, the reformatory and the insane asylum," he said, "all represented an effort to ensure cohesion of the community in new and changing circumstances."[52]

Rothman further analyzed the purpose of these institutions as both shelter and rehabilitation. Antebellum reformers believed that family government had broken down and in many cases, children were not being imbued with proper notions of right and wrong. This problem was compounded by environmental considerations. Without a strong sense of authority and moral government, it was simply too easy for individuals to fall prey to assorted vices. Since most asylum advocates had jettisoned Calvinistic assumptions regarding humanity's inherent sinfulness and adopted a more malleable view of the individual, they believed waywards were not beyond hope. By carefully regulating asylum environments and providing all inmates with the same strict, disciplined schedule, asylum advocates believed they could rehabilitate society's lawbreakers.[53]

Unfortunately, these institutions did not fulfill the dreams of their idealistic planners. Asylums gradually lost their rehabilitation emphasis and became either instruments of punishment or merely places to dump society's dispossessed. Moreover, in this transition to custodialism, some argue that asylums became tools of the middle class to impose social control on people who were potential threats to social stability. In examining the Home Missionary Society of Philadelphia and the Children's Aid Society in Pennsylvania, for instance, Priscilla Ferguson Clement maintains that while both groups had a humanitarian impulse, both actively sought to provide orphans with disciplined, well-maintained environments, preferably in individual homes, so they would become better citizens.[54] Clement also notes, "They were concerned less with the individual, personal problems of the children than they were with the social moral problems he or she posed in the larger community."[55]

In some ways Baptist orphanages in the late nineteenth and early twentieth centuries were similar to antebellum asylums. Both sought to provide sheltered environments for those dwelling therein. Both emphasized the importance of strong, internal, moral self-government.

Such facilities were to serve as socializing institutions in the absence of an established family structure.[56]

Beyond this there are few similarities. Rothman's asylum builders were confident that their institutions, at least in their early stages, could solve society's problems. Antebellum orphanages were built upon the supposition that, if left to themselves, parentless children would naturally slip into debauchery. Hence, the primary function of antebellum orphanages had been to prevent children from becoming juvenile delinquents by providing both discipline and rehabilitation. "On a manner clearly reminiscent of the mental hospital and the penitentiary, and to some degree of the almshouse as well," Rothman argues, "they expected to demonstrate the validity of general principles through the specific treatment of deviants and dependents."[57]

Baptists viewed orphanhood as a much stickier problem than did their antebellum predecessors. They believed that nothing, including adoption, could solve the problems created by parental loss. Orphanhood's negative effects, however, could be blunted if their institutions provided a strong familylike structure and Christian education. They did not believe that orphans needed rehabilitation. Further, they did not seek to impose a uniform method of treatment for all orphaned children for whom they cared. Baptists envisioned their orphanages in much broader terms than mere custodial repositories for society's dispossessed. As they saw it, orphans had lost their parents, a problem that no one could solve. By providing surrogate parent figures and grouping orphans together, they believed it was possible to re-create an adequate family structure. Orphans may have lost their *parents*, but it did not necessarily follow that they had lost their *home*.

There is evidence suggesting that Baptist orphanages self-consciously sought to distance themselves from other orphanages. A. T. Jamison was perhaps the most articulate critic of institutional orphan care, and he serves as a good example of Baptist childcare thought. He believed it was detrimental for children to receive "uniform treatment." He believed that every child should be treated as an individual and allowed to develop a degree of self-expression and self-determination. "It is easy for the management to lay down iron-clad rules as to conduct and require every child to conform thereto," he observed. "This would be justified if all children were created exactly alike. But they are very unlike and each has his own individuality to develop."[58]

Throughout his career at the Connie Maxwell Home, Jamison insisted that parentless children were "just as good" as any other. He wanted to avoid orphaned children seeing themselves as a class distinct from other children. "Happy are we," he insisted, "if we keep our children from developing class consciousness."[59]

This emphasis on individualism led Jamison to believe that children had certain rights regardless of whether or not they had living parents. Structurally, each child deserved a clean dwelling place to call home, with an abundance of light and the love of either a mother or foster mother. Each child had a right to his or her own bed and adequate toilet facilities. Each child also had the right to pure water, good food—not necessarily gourmet, but appetizing—and one quart of milk per day. Children also had the right to their own personal clothing and instruction in personal hygiene. Finally, Jamison argued that each child had certain social rights, including education that was both practical and religious/moral. Above all, he believed that each child should be treated as an individual.[60]

Implementing these rights in an institutional context was expensive, and Jamison cautioned against excessive frugality. He saw real problems when institutions sought the cheapest, as opposed to the best, means of addressing children's personal needs. This was especially true of hiring housemothers. Jamison believed each orphan deserved a home, but admitted the problem of one "mother" caring for twenty-five children in a building that was not constructed to meet their needs.[61]

In spite of this, Jamison was still confident that Baptist orphanages were superior to orphan asylums. The thing that made them better was the homelike quality they tried to create. Each Home had its own distinct daily routine, and Baptists made no secret of their desire to lead their orphans into "useful citizenship." Nevertheless, there is little evidence suggesting middle-class manipulation with a view to social control. Two things are particularly telling in this regard. First, Baptists did not see orphans as delinquents needing rehabilitation. Second, the fact that Baptists viewed each child as an individual suggests that they had no preconceived "social norm" to superimpose on the children. It is true that children in Baptist orphanages received religious instruction and attended Baptist churches. It is also true that orphanage officials were delighted when their "family members" joined a Baptist church. Jamison noted that the church on the Connie Maxwell grounds had established such groups as the Baptist Young People's Training Unions and Royal Ambassadors to furnish a working knowledge of Southern Baptist denominational life. He believed this would enable them to take their own place in a community and a local church with a knowledge of "what is expected of them and what has to be done."[62] Clearly, children in Baptist orphanages were groomed for continued denominational activity after their discharge. Orphanage officials did not force children into either conversion or church membership, but they hoped that upon leaving the orphanage each child would lead a life that reflected the moral precepts he or she learned at the Home. In 1904, R. C. Buckner proudly noted that his former "children" had entered the workforce in a variety of occupations but none ran a saloon or "gambling house."[63]

While Baptists did not see their orphanages as rehabilitation centers, they did appreciate the fact that such centers existed. In 1899, George Farnham, president of the Board of Trustees for Alabama's Orphanage, noted that the state had just built a reform school for boys and argued that it was better to send "problem children" to reform school than to an orphanage. "We have found from experience that it is a very bad policy to send children of that class to this Home because their bad influence has a very deleterious effect upon the disciplines and morals of the entire Home," he declared, "and we cannot be too careful along this line."[64]

There is also evidence suggesting that Baptist orphanages did not receive severely crippled or mentally retarded children. In assessing North Carolina's orphanage, Bernard Washington Spilman noted that while the Home's founder, John Haynes Mills, was sympathetic to the needs of the handicapped, he did not feel that an orphanage was the proper place for them. He therefore called on the state to build a school for the feebleminded. Spilman disgustedly wrote, "The people of the state could not be stampeded about anything. They were not in any hurry. North Carolina lost its opportunity to vote for George Washington for President of the United States because it was in no hurry to enter the Union."[65]

What were denominational institutions to do when faced with such challenges? The Alabama and North Carolina examples indicate that when these Homes perceived they had reached a limit to their ministry, their administrators sought to demonstrate the need for other public institutions. This was especially true regarding juvenile delinquents. Baptists cared about these children, too, but they did not believe they were equipped to address their specific problems. Neither did they want unruly children to disrupt the homelike environment they were trying to create. Besides, these issues clearly involved no Biblical mandate for Baptists to use to justify such actions.

The problem of juvenile delinquency poses an interesting point. Baptists were curiously silent about the problems from which their charges had been delivered or that they would face upon leaving the Home. Rothman's asylum builders read such advisory volumes as Lydia Child's *The Mother's Book* and Catherine Beecher's *A Treatise on Domestic Economy for Young Ladies at Home.* Many such authors saw society in crisis terms because they equated socioeconomic change with declension, and Rothman dubs them a "nervous group."[66] Baptists, however, wrote little concerning the world's anxiety. Doubtless they deplored houses of prostitution, gambling, public drunkenness, and the like. Yet, they did not appear to fear such influences on their children, perhaps because they were too concerned with their children's formative years to worry about past influences or potential future evil. It may also be that orphanage administrators and workers believed the training their children received would adequately equip them to handle the pressures and temptations they would encounter in the world.

These Southern Baptist orphanages tried to provide the best possible medical care and education for their children. They also tried to provide a homelike atmosphere that gave orphaned children, in addition to mere shelter, a sense of stability and community. And in the process, they wanted to make the children into better citizens. Likewise, the commitment to aid children in their mental as well as spiritual development suggests that Baptist social concern was much deeper than simply mass evangelism. Baptists could find a Biblical mandate to minister to orphans; they could not find a corresponding mandate for education.

Considered together, these actions provide evidence that Baptist concern for the South's needy, especially orphaned children, extended beyond mere charity. But, assessing the point where charity ceases to be charity and becomes something broader is no easy matter. Relieving poverty-stricken, destitute people may be seen as charity. Is the Baptist orphanage movement between 1890 and 1920 merely charity writ large? The answer must be no. There are several reasons for this.

Late nineteenth- and early twentieth-century Baptists in the South were becoming increasingly self-conscious of their potential to both evangelize and effect social change. In addition to evangelical fervor, this self-awareness manifested itself in denominational activities such as building permanent institutions to assist orphans.

In building orphanages, however, Southern Baptists did more than simply institutionalize their benevolence. Baptist orphanages gave everyone, rich and poor, the opportunity to participate in missionary activity that would benefit an easily identifiable and vulnerable group. As Mississippi Baptists asserted in 1914, "Many benevolent institutions depend upon the specially interested or the wealthy few, while our Orphanage depends entirely upon the voluntary offering of the many."[67] Between 1890 and 1920, any Southern Baptist orphanage could have articulated the same sentiment. These institutions offered the opportunity to express compassion for the less fortunate. And Baptists could do so with confidence that they had both God's sanction and commandment.

Most significant, one must view these institutions not only from how and what Baptists gave to them but also for what they did for the children. Between 1890 and 1920, Baptists increasingly committed funding to this aspect of denominational work. This cooperative spirit, teamed with the objectives of the individual homes, indicates that rather than engaging in mere charity, Baptists were synthesizing their evangelical fervor with their social concern. Their attitude toward orphans demonstrates that Southern Baptists possessed the ability to transcend a narrow, evangelistic ethos for a broader, more enthusiastic approach to a pressing social problem.

5

REDEEMING THE MOUNTAINEERS
Southern Baptists and
Mountain Mission Schools

"The fear of the LORD is the beginning of knowledge: but fools despise wisdom and instruction."

Proverbs 1:7

"Through knowledge shall the just be delivered."

Proverbs 11:9b

EDUCATION REFORM was a staple theme of American reformers between 1890 and 1920. Dewey Grantham notes that education reform touched more lives than any other aspect of southern social reform during the Progressive Era. In addition to opening the door for northern philanthropic interests, he argues, "it [education reform] was almost always viewed by reformers as a redemptive force in the development of a better South."[1] Additionally, Grantham maintains that southern churches were instrumental in furnishing this era with a humanitarian spirit. "The clergy," he writes, "spoke out with greater frequency against social evils, religious bodies showed a deepening interest in the improvement of social conditions, and all of the major Protestant denominations established social action agencies of one kind or another."[2]

Southern Baptists were particularly zealous to build schools in southern mountain regions, and between 1890 and 1920, the Home Mission Board aided numerous schools and colleges in the Appalachian and Ozark mountains. These mountain schools provided what may be the best example of the Baptist synthesis of social concern and missionary enterprise. On the one hand, Baptists wanted to use these schools to provide training for mountain ministers. On the other hand, they could claim no Biblical mandate to build schools that provided "secular" education. Their ambition to furnish mountain children with an education, therefore, needs further investigation.

While Southern Baptists built or assisted numerous mountain schools between 1890 and 1920, they were not the first religious group that tried to educate mountaineers. In *Appalachia on Our Mind,* Henry D. Shapiro argues that after the Civil War, northern Protestant missionary agencies quickly moved into mountainous areas of the South because they saw potential gains for their various denominations. They created an ideology that stressed Appalachian "otherness." They believed that mountaineers had been particularly isolated from mainstream American life and consequently lacked the institutions they most needed for socialization—churches and schools.[3] Moreover, they articulated the differences they perceived between Appalachia and America as social problems that could be cured through education and religion. "If these were provided," Shapiro noted, "then the mountaineer could literally be 'uplifted' into modern American life, and that danger to American homogeneity and unity implicit in the very existence of 'exceptional populations' be eliminated."[4]

As Shapiro observed, northern missionaries emphasized uplift for mountaineers through education. Such terminology was also common among Southern Baptist thinkers and educators. The Baptist Press, particularly the Home Mission Board's *Our Home Field,* never concealed its delight that graduates from mountain schools made significant contributions to their respective communities. Nevertheless, Baptists resented what they perceived as a smug, arrogant assessment of mountaineers on behalf of northern missionaries, which Shapiro describes as "Appalachian otherness." One writer accused northern missionary agents of exaggerating mountain ignorance and cultural dissimilarities between mountain people and northern urbanites. "The missionary literature on the whole," he said, "is an exploitation of missionary effect."[5] He further argued that the touchstone for assessing mountaineer "ignorance, poverty, or loneliness" should not be "that of Beacon Street."[6]

While Southern Baptists may have resented northern cultural condescension, an examination of the mountain schools they built or assisted reveals that they had their own agenda. They agreed with their northern brethren that Appalachia was a distinct part of the South and that mountaineers had their own particular problems. Yet Southern Baptists built mountain schools on two basic assumptions. First, they believed mountain people had descended from pure Anglo-Saxon stock. Consequently, they were victims of geographic circumstances, in that rugged mountain terrain had hindered their building churches and schools. Without such socializing institutions, these white mountaineers needed help. John White, a representative of the Home Mission Board, made the racial bias clear when he said mountain "backwardness" was not due to "ancestral degeneracy" or "stubborn racial background."[7] Baptist mountain schools were meant to uplift whites only.

The second foundation for these schools rested on New South economic boosterism. John White saw sweeping changes coming to the mountains. He noted that Appalachia possessed tremendous wealth in coal, iron ore, and various metals, as well as timber and abundant water to power machinery. In addition, railroads were making travel easier, rendering mountaineers less isolated. The question was, What would mountain people do in the face of socioeconomic upheaval? White believed that education was essential to ushering mountaineers into the modern world.[8]

Attacking southern education woes at the turn of the century was not easy. Progressive education reformers struggled against the tightfistedness of post-Reconstruction Bourbonism. By 1890, the lack of an adequate tax base had left an indelible mark on southern schools. In Alabama, schools suffered because the state legislature was unwilling to spend money on public education. Additionally, an 1890 tax cut left little revenue for public education, and local towns began levying taxes to support schools. In 1895, St. Clair County levied a ten-cent tax for education. Walker County followed suit in 1896, as did Lamar and Fayette counties in 1899.[9] Alabama's problems were not exceptional. In 1887, Tennessee had only four secondary schools, and its primary schools met sporadically.[10]

Such fiscal frugality inevitably led to low salaries for teachers and scarcely any furnishings for the school building. For example, in 1900–1901 the average Kentucky teacher earned $34.10 per month. Black teachers earned only $29.95 per month.[11] Things were scarcely better in North Carolina, where in 1916, white teachers earned $40.74 per month, while black teachers earned $24.69.[12] Such figures are not surprising in light of the fact that in 1900 the national average expenditure per pupil was $2.84. Southern expenditures per pupil ranged from a low of $.50 in Arkansas and North Carolina to a high of $1.72 in Oklahoma.[13] School buildings tended to have only one room, where all grades met together. Teaching aids were sometimes limited to chalk and blackboard erasers, alphabet charts, a dictionary, a globe, and a few maps.[14]

It was difficult to recruit teachers under such poor circumstances, and many who entered the classroom were either unqualified or unconcerned with their students' progress. Some students complained that teachers arrived late, left early, and napped throughout the day. Others recalled teachers who left students unattended while they tended to personal business.[15]

To further compound matters, the South's rural population was spread so thinly that it was almost impossible to build centrally located schools. In 1900, seven southern states had a rural population of between 70 and 80 percent, while six states had a rural population of between 80 and 90 percent.[16] In Alabama, the Elbridge Academy was more than twenty-five miles away from the next closest school in Jasper.[17] "Clearly then," as William Dabney notes, "universal public education could never succeed in these states unless the schools in the county were made more efficient."[18]

These factors contributed to a high illiteracy rate among southerners. In 1900, only 6.2 percent of the nation's white population ten years or older was illiterate. It was a different story in the South, where only four states—Florida, Mississippi, Texas, and Oklahoma—could boast an illiteracy rate of less than 10 percent. Louisiana's and North Carolina's illiteracy rates were 18.4 percent and 19.4 percent, respectively.[19]

It is clear that, between 1890 and 1920, southern states needed schools and teachers. With money and equipment for public schools in short supply, concerned parents looked to alternative means for educating their children. Private schools and academies, particularly those maintained by religious agencies, were attractive options.

Despite lofty intentions, Baptists were slow to develop mountain schools, but it was not because they lacked desire. As early as 1885,

I. T. Tichenor, Corresponding Secretary of the Home Mission Board, noted that the Board supported some twelve missionaries in the western Carolinas. Their missionaries had enjoyed some success, but Tichenor lamented their lack of spiritual and intellectual development. Nevertheless, he predicted that in the future the world would experience both the power and strength of mountain people as they developed their natural resources.[20]

Over the next several years Tichenor annually reminded his fellow Southern Baptists of the great, yet undeveloped, educational potential mountain children possessed. Yet in 1891, Baptist involvement in educational work was limited to the Home Mission Board's subsidizing the principal's salary at Hiawasee Institute in Georgia.[21]

This limited participation continued throughout the 1890s until 1897. In that year the North Carolina Baptists met in convention at Morganton. They learned that the Presbyterians conceded that the majority of mountain people were affiliated with Baptist churches. Nevertheless, since Baptists were not providing educational opportunities for their own people, Presbyterians saw an opportunity to expand their own work in that area.[22]

Messengers to the Southern Baptist Convention in 1898 discussed the need for some means by which they could advance education for mountaineers. The Convention appointed Dr. John E. White to investigate the question and to begin looking for someone to supervise Baptist educational undertakings in the mountains. In 1900, White reported that the Presbyterians were indeed building schools in the mountains, and he urged Baptists to rise to this challenge. In an impassioned plea he told his brethren that the denomination that provided the mountains with educational opportunities would "shape permanently the religious, social, and denominational character of the mountain people."[23]

White then proposed that Southern Baptists commit their resources to establishing schools in the Appalachian mountains. Under White's plan the Home Mission Board would work in cooperation with the state boards in those states with mountainous territory. The program aimed to acquaint mountain churches with the Southern Baptist Convention and its various state conventions, to train young ministers, and to provide mountain youths with educational opportunities and encourage some even to go on to college. Of course, such schools needed to be "located strategically" and be supervised whenever possible by the cooperative efforts of several Baptist associations. Moreover, under this plan each school was to have a Bible teacher who would not only teach Bible-related material but also spend Saturdays and Sundays visiting area churches and instructing them in such areas as missionary giving, the potential of education, and all-around church duties.[24]

Clearly, Southern Baptists saw such schools as an opportunity to extend Baptist faith and practice into the Appalachians. One of the main purposes of these schools was to train ministers to preach in mountain pulpits. Also, since these schools included Bible courses in their curriculum, teachers used this opportunity to evangelize their pupils. In some cases, as will be discussed later, children who were converted in school were instrumental in their parents' conversion; yet these schools had an impact beyond religious conversions. White specifically told the Southern Baptist Convention that such schools should provide children with a background that would prepare them for collegiate study. Such an education would prepare mountain children for "the work of life, the duties of citizenship, and usefulness as Christians."[25]

Having convinced his fellow Baptists that such an endeavor was both necessary and feasible, White's next problem was finding someone to head the project. He finally settled on Albert E. Brown, assistant corresponding secretary of the North Carolina Baptist State Convention. Brown served the Home Mission Board as the first Superintendent of the Department of Mountain Schools and was the driving force behind Southern Baptist educational endeavors in the mountains until his death in 1924. He was well equipped to serve his constituency in both a ministerial and educational capacity. His father, William Albert Gallatin Brown, was the first president of Mars Hill College, Mars Hill, North Carolina. Moreover, he had four siblings, all of whom were teachers and three of whom were ordained ministers.[26]

Brown was converted as a sixteen-year-old student at Carson-Newman College in Jefferson City, Tennessee. He did not enter the ministry until his brother Dudley's death in 1889. Dudley Brown had been pastor of Berea Baptist Church near Swannanoa, North Carolina. With the pulpit vacant, Albert Brown volunteered his services to the church, and they were accepted. Among those present on his first Sunday was

Miss Osie Allison, who later recalled that Dudley Brown's death had influenced Albert's decision to enter the ministry. He told the congregation, "Brethren and friends, I am Dudley Brown's brother—I have fought the call. God has taken my brother to show me that I am not doing my duty. I am now ready to assume the call, if you will consider me in Dudley's place."[27]

Brown was subsequently ordained and served the North Carolina Baptists in numerous capacities until John E. White urged him to get involved in educating mountain children. Initially, Brown resisted the idea, but White's persistence paid dividends. In 1899, Brown left the pastorate, but it was not until July 1904 that the Home Mission Board recognized him as the Superintendent of Mountain Mission Schools at a salary of $1,200 per year plus travel expenses.[28] Using Brown's salary as a measure of his worth to the Home Mission Board, it is noteworthy that in January 1906, he received $1,500 per year plus expenses. That salary was adjusted to $2,000 per year in 1907, and in 1912, A. E. Brown received $2,500 per year. These figures represent salary only; Brown's expenses were also paid by the Board.[29] There is some justification for the confidence reflected by these salary increases. After only one year, the Home Board indicated that attendance in the existing mountain schools had increased by 20 percent from the previous year.[30] The exact figures that indicate this increase are not available. Nevertheless, a 20-percent increase in enrollment is significant, and Brown's work in Mountain Mission Schools was just beginning.

If Brown was initially reluctant to become Superintendent of Mountain Mission Schools, he quickly formed a concept of his duty upon accepting his new position. In July 1904, he offered the Home Mission Board a description of how he planned to operate the Mountain Mission Schools, subject to their approval. Brown left no doubt that the Mountain Mission Schools would serve in a dual capacity of evangelizing and educating. Brown also insisted that he would work in harmony with state mission boards and state educational societies whenever possible and that such work would be confined strictly to the South's mountainous regions. Likewise, as Chief Administrator of Mountain Mission Schools, he saw himself as one who would advise the Board regarding particular school needs, and he believed he should look for schools that the Home Mission Board could assist. Brown believed he should even develop ties with Baptist colleges for the purpose of recruiting teachers for the Mountain Mission Schools. As he carried out the functions of his office, Brown promised he would make regular monthly reports to the Board and serve the denomination in a broad sense according to the "general interests of the Board."[31]

The Board agreed with Brown, and he officially began his work as Superintendent of Mountain Mission Schools in July 1904. It was not long before some institutions that were not located in the mountains solicited aid from the Home Mission Board, as did an unnamed school in 1909. The response was negative, and the Board cited three reasons:

1. That our mountain school problem is naturally confined to the mountain regions geographically and this confinement should be emphasized by the Board.
2. That the Superintendent, Rev. A. E. Brown, has reached the limits of physical possibility in his supervisory labors and as an extension of his field will require expert assistance not now available.
3. That the limited financial resources of the Board requires the recognition of the limitation of appropriations to Mountain Mission and School work to almost absolute necessities of the schools already in our system.[32]

The first portion of the Board's response is significant. The Home Mission Board limited its educational work to the mountains because of the "mountain school problem." The Baptists believed that mountaineers were more prone to ignorance and poverty than were those in other areas of the South. Equally clear is the fact that A. E. Brown and the Home Mission Board believed this ignorance and poverty were not insurmountable. With the proper attention Baptists could provide education for mountain people and even see increases in their own congregations.

By 1920, Mountain Missions aided some forty-one schools on a regular basis. Of that number eight were in North Carolina and Tennessee, five were in Georgia and Kentucky, and four were in South Carolina and Alabama.[33] In 1912, the Southern Baptists investigated the possibility of assisting schools in the Ozark Mountains. The Ozarks are not in the same proximity as the Appalachias, and the Home Board was thus initially reluctant to support such schools.[34] They finally gave in, however, and by 1920, they were assisting five schools in Arkansas and one in Missouri.

Mountain Mission School, East Tennessee, circa 1920. (Courtesy of the Southern Baptist Historical Library and Archives, Historical Commission, SBC, Nashville, Tennessee.)

Receiving aid from the Home Board was not as difficult as it might appear, but there were preconditions that all schools were required to meet to receive Southern Baptist support. First, schools applying for assistance had to be recommended by the state mission board of the state in which the institution was located. The school's trustee board, or a similar group, was to hold the title to the facilities in fee simple. Then, regardless of a school's curriculum, the Home Mission Board required all institutions it supported to offer courses in Bible and missions. Moreover, the trustees were to encourage especially promising young ministers to receive their education by offering them free tuition. Finally, each institution was required to submit regular reports to the Home Mission Board.[35]

Occasionally the Home Board made lump-sum apportionments to state mission boards without specifying the sums or specific schools to be assisted. Such was the case in 1903 when the Home Board gave the state of Tennessee $1,100 for education. In other instances, the Board assisted state mission boards in a slightly different manner. For example, in 1899, the Board agreed to help Mr. M. A. Wilson and the

Reverends D. A. Ramey and C. A. Jones, all from Virginia. The Board agreed to pay each man $200 a year, while the Virginia Home Mission Board paid each man $100 per year. A more common scenario, however, was for schools that had originally begun as independent academies to solicit the Home Mission Board for assistance. For example, Christopher Columbus Choat converted to Christianity when he was 62 years old. In 1909, he and his son-in-law founded Stockton's Valley Institute. The two men bore the school's expenses for its first year, but the financial drain and local apathy were too great a burden. Choat wanted the Home Board to assume control of the school, and in 1911 upon A. E. Brown's recommendation, it did.[36]

Other denominations were also interested in educating mountain children. Besides Baptists, Presbyterians actively promoted mountain schools, and Baptists were particularly fond of using them as benchmarks for measuring their own progress. In 1909, Dr. John E. White informed the Home Mission Board that the Presbyterians maintained fifty mountain schools, whereas the Baptists had only twenty-six. The Presbyterians, however, boasted only 3,906 students, while the Baptists had 4,516. White also noted that in the previous year the Presbyterian Board had appropriated $118,000, as compared to $28,000 by the Baptists. This represented an average appropriation of $30.20 per pupil for the Presbyterians and $6.20 for the Baptists. With a degree of pride White noted, "This is to say that it costs our Presbyterian brethren $24 more per pupil to do school work in the mountains than it does Southern Baptists."[37] He noted further that the Presbyterians averaged only three teachers per school while the Baptists averaged five, and the Presbyterians concentrated on kindergarten and primary education while the Baptists focused on secondary and college education.[38]

Beyond mere per-pupil spending, these figures represent differing basic philosophies. On the one hand, the Presbyterians maintained their schools with funds acquired outside of the mountains. The Baptists argued that such practices encouraged pauperism and did not encourage local communities to pay for their own schools. On the other hand, Baptists could not educate children any more cheaply than their Presbyterian counterparts. The difference, however, lay in the fact that Baptists charged higher tuition rates and called upon local communities to help support their own schools.[39] They were successful in this practice, and it had several benefits, not the least of which was allowing the Home Board to spread its meager resources thin. By not concentrating aid to any particular institution they were able to help more schools, thereby maximizing resources. Additionally, the Baptists believed their philosophy fostered greater community involvement. That is, when people supported a school in their community they committed themselves *both* to the school and to the community. The Baptist philosophy also emphasized self-help and minimized dependence on funding outside the mountain region. Nevertheless, White lamented that for the 153 counties he identified as "mountain," there were only twenty-six schools, or roughly one school for each seven counties.[40]

Despite the fact that there were only twenty-six schools in 1909, both the Home Mission Board and A. E. Brown were pleased that mountain people had contributed the majority of his budget. He noted that in 1908, his total expenditure for equipment was $96,290. All but $12,000 of this sum had been donated by the mountaineers themselves.[41]

Much of the credit for such generosity lies with Brown himself. He had originally seen himself as both an administrator and a fundraiser. Brown was gifted in both areas, but he was particularly innovative in financing his mountain schools. He addressed churches and communities and was never ashamed to plead his cause. On one occasion he preached "on the head of Cosby Creek in the mountains." There was a mountain school in this community, but it suffered from a lack of funding. Brown announced that on Monday afternoon he would meet with all interested citizens regarding the school and its finances. He later recalled, "At this meeting I raised $1,001, securing a subscription from everyone present in the house."[42]

Brown's knack for fundraising notwithstanding, the mountain people also deserve some credit for wanting the education Brown offered. This is especially apparent in one episode with the "Hardshell Baptists," which Brown related to *Our Home Field*. The Hardshells disagreed with many facets of the Southern Baptist program, especially Sunday schools, missionary agencies, and paid clergymen.[43] At any rate, Brown attended a meeting of Hardshell Baptists and told them of the Home Mission Board's effort to establish schools in the mountains. He appealed to them as both a mountaineer and a fellow Baptist. The Hardshells invited him to preach, and Brown seized the opportunity. He preached two messages, both of which discussed missions, Sunday school education, and ministerial support. Brown ultimately convinced the Hardshells that his position was sound.[44]

By avoiding doctrinal differences and emphasizing those areas where they agreed, especially the economic potential in the mountains and the benefits of general education, Brown reaffirmed something these people already knew—they needed schools. Yet denominational concern for mountain regions as "needy" areas hinged on a variety of factors. True, they wanted to see more churches in the mountains, and they wanted to furnish educational opportunities for mountain people. Behind this motivation, however, was the assumption that white mountaineers were particularly "worthy" of aid. In 1900, when John E. White told the Southern Baptist Convention of his desire to see schools built in the mountains, he stressed what he termed the "quality of native stock" in the mountains, 98 percent of whom were "pure Caucasian." He further noted that they were a religious people, but needed religious education. Missions and missionary schools were the answer, he said, and whoever provided those would shape the mountaineer character.[45]

Another author noted that Appalachians had fought bravely in the American Revolution, and because of such heroism and heritage they deserved to have better schools and more preachers. Besides, Mormon missionaries had begun to evangelize Appalachia, and the writer could not bear to think of the consequences if such practices were not checked. Baptists had to act quickly to mount an evangelical counter-offensive of sorts. Mountaineers needed schools and churches to alert people to the "artful insinuations and . . . pernicious doctrines and practices" of all unorthodox interlopers.[46]

Even A. E. Brown believed that mountaineers were worthy of special evangelization. He felt mountaineers were suffering from what he perceived as undeveloped potential. Many churches paid their pastors a paltry fifteen or twenty dollars a year, a fact that demonstrated to Brown ignorance of a church's duty to its pastor.[47] Brown also believed mountaineers deserved special attention because of who they were. He said mountain people were "pure Americans who are descendants of the original settlers of Virginia and the Carolinas; in religion they are evangelical; they are white people; a rural country people; and they are a Baptist people."[48]

The implications here are clear. Baptist leaders saw the mountains as an area where they had a mandate to extend their influence. Mountain people were being evangelized by Presbyterians and Mormons, among others. Nevertheless, these people had Baptist roots and "pure" Anglo-Saxon bloodlines. Moreover, due to the rough mountain terrain, these people had been deprived of the opportunities to receive an education and forge the community ties that other southerners enjoyed. Oscar M. Drennen's testimonial helps illustrate this point. Drennen said he had been interested in school at an early age, but in his fifth year he and his teacher did not get along. He found reasons to avoid school, and finally dropped out. He began working as a logger, and his life was filled with "struggles and battles." Drennen did not specify the exact nature of these conflicts, but he did note that he remained uninterested in education. His conversion to Christianity, however, made him realize "the opportunities in the world [?] for those who prepare for efficient service." He entered the Harrison-Chilaowee Institute on December 28, 1908, and finished in 1915.[49] From his testimonial it is clear that Drennen believed the twin influences of religion and education were beneficial. Not only did he desire to serve God "efficiently," but he also wanted to take advantage of the "opportunities" available to him.

There is also evidence to suggest that teachers in the schools shared many of the same attitudes their administrators held. One teacher, Miss Osie Allison, served in numerous capacities in the mountain schools. She was converted at age nine and joined the Berea Baptist Church, near Swannanoa, North Carolina. Writing in October 1927, she said, "I was not only fortunate in having Christian parents but in having the best of pastors—pastors who were educated and progressive."[50]

A. E. Brown had been one of Miss Allison's pastors and in 1901 asked her to teach at the Haywood Institute in Clyde, North Carolina. The Mountain Missions and Schools program was in its infancy, and scarcely any teacher knew what to expect. Academically, there was little difference between state and mission schools. Funding was likewise a problem for both. A. E. Brown, however, saw a difference. He wanted teachers in the schools to be imbued with a certain esprit de corps that elevated the role of "teacher" to something higher. Brown wanted mission schoolteachers to see themselves as uplifters of mountaineers. Allison recalled, "I think very few, if any, of the teachers had really caught the vision."[51] It was not long before Allison "caught the vision." She taught at Clyde for two years before leaving for the Yancey Collegiate Institute at Burnville, North Carolina. It was there, she noted, that she saw the real benefit of Christian schools. Burnville was a small town, Allison observed, and many children "were allowed a great deal of freedom. Many did not know Christ in the home. You can readily see why the school meant so much to the younger generation, the hope of the country."[52]

Allison also noted that teachers in the mountain schools suffered hardships and discouragements that "only a mountain teacher knows." While at the Yancey Institute she recalled that at one point the school had 200 pupils and only four teachers. When one teacher left in the middle of the first term, three teachers were left to handle the students.[53] She also remembered certain foreign missionaries who had visited the mountain schools and, comparing them to similar institutions in foreign lands, noted that the foreign schools were "better equipped and the dormitories more comfortable" than those in the mountain schools.[54]

Despite the spartan accommodations, Allison noted that the hardships of teaching in a mountain school were minimal when one considered the benefits. She relished the idea that she had played a role in educating mountain youth. It was easy to forget hardship and discouragement, she observed, when she thought that she and her fellow teachers "had some small part in helping to form the ideals of some of these [students]."[55] In helping furnish an education for Appalachian youth, not only had she assisted her denomination, but she had also provided a basis from which they could serve Christ more effectively. But education meant much more. She noted that "it means a more highly educated class of men and women; it means better citizenship throughout our country; it means more Christian homes."[56] The implication is obvious. The better one prepared his or herself to serve God, the more prepared they would be to function in society. They would espouse Christian ethical assumptions such as brotherly love, and they would obey the laws of the land. Southern Baptists had no master plan to shape society. They clearly believed that any attempt to make society better, whether the issue was social justice in the abstract or obeying civil law, had to begin with the individual.

East Tennessee Missionary Work among Children. (Courtesy of the Southern Baptist Historical Library and Archives, Historical Commission, SBC, Nashville, Tennessee.)

A. E. Brown shared similar sentiments. In 1911, he noted that over the past dozen years the mountain schools had made an impact on Appalachian society. "The moral tone has greatly improved," he said, "crime has lessened, feuds have disappeared, respect for law inculcated."[57]

Additionally, he noted that local churches were stronger, local prohibition sentiment was greater, and local public schools benefited from mountain school graduates who taught there. He also believed home life had improved for many.[58] Brown did not specify what he meant by improved home life, but obviously believed Christianity benefited all homes. He did note that many homes had built guest chambers with bureaus, washbowls, and other "conveniences." This, he said, demonstrated the "response of mountain people to advanced ideas of home life."[59]

Brown was also pleased that the mountain schools were well received in their communities. In 1906, he informed *Our Home Field* that the teachers were grasping the potential impact such schools could have and that some schools were so crowded that many students could not enroll.[60] Less than one year later he wrote of the "embarrassment" of having to deal with teachers who were pleading for larger facilities. Sadly, he said, "To turn away boys and girls who have a fierce eagerness for that training which will lift them out of their present spheres is little better than a crime, or so our teachers feel."[61]

Baptists felt compelled to meet the challenge posed by the "fierce eagerness" mountain children displayed for education. Gauging their success is difficult; establishing a link between Mountain Mission Schools and Progressive assumptions is not. Dewey W. Grantham has suggested that the regulatory impulse and the drive for social justice were among the most important Progressive Era campaigns. Regulators emphasized reform, especially political and penal reform. Social justice, however, was broader and included child labor legislation, education, and organized charity. The driving force behind social justice, he suggested, was social efficiency.[62] He also argued that most Progressive Era campaigns assumed a regional flavor whereby progressives could tout them as "southern" reforms. "In other words," he said, "progressives were able to create a strong sense of community as a setting for their pursuit of social reform."[63]

Baptist evangelical zeal merged with a strong sense of family to build institutions that benefited numerous local communities. Brown's reports to the Home Mission Board stressed the value of the mountain schools. In addition to fulfilling the evangelical element of bringing about their conversion, they were also strengthening their local communities by training and graduating students who submitted themselves to local laws. Additionally, since local communities were largely responsible for maintaining schools, these same communities had to work together in order to keep the schools functioning. This doubtless helped create stronger community ties.

This concern to create strong community ties was based on paternalism. Baptist leadership believed that poor mountaineers were culturally isolated and, hence, needed to be ushered into the modern world. Implicit in this assumption was another one that maintained that with the proper sort of help, mountaineers would do well for themselves and their children. Victor Masters briefly noted, "Their number is millions. Their blood is the most pure Anglo-Saxon blood in America. Their habits and manners are simple; *they are like chil-*

dren."[64] He further noted, "What a vast opportunity is there [in the mountains]. Evangelized, but not developed, converted but untrained, their pure need is education under strictly Christian influences."[65]

Baptist missionary schools also reflect the progressive drive for social efficiency. For example, A. E. Brown was selected to oversee the mountain schools largely because of his background. Stated simply, he was a native of western North Carolina and had served the churches of that area. He was the individual best suited for this job because he was himself a mountaineer and could readily identify with mountain needs. Mountaineers could also identify with Brown for the same reasons. Much like their counterparts in the business community, Baptists wanted the "best man for the job."[66] In this case Brown was best suited to lead in educating mountain children.

This drive for efficiency extended beyond Mountain Mission School leadership. One of the main reasons for building mountain schools was to help prepare mountain people to meet the challenges of a changing economic structure. Southern Baptist leaders foresaw changes in the southern economy. They believed the region would soon be rich. They also believed that they should use their money wisely as good servants of God. By spreading their resources thinly, Southern Baptist leaders believed they were instilling self-reliance within their constituency. True, some were ambivalent about the future. In 1910, A. E. Brown expressed his fear that unless Appalachian resources were managed wisely, the land would lose the wealth that should benefit mountaineers.[67] In the meanwhile, however, he wanted to see Appalachian children receive both the religious training and education they deserved. True to his Progressive roots, Brown doubtless believed these two keys would open a new door in mountain spirituality, culture, and well-being.

Finally, one of the most regrettable features of southern Progressivism was that it did little for blacks. One historian has suggested that Progressivism was "For Whites Only."[68] This is painfully evident in the notion that mountaineers were worthy of assistance because they were "pure Anglo-Saxon stock." Baptists missed a great opportunity to minister to blacks at the turn of the century, and the next chapter will explore some of the reasons for this.

6

OF LEOPARD SPOTS
AND ETHIOPIAN SKIN
Southern Baptists and Racial Uplift

"Can the Ethiopian change his skin, or the leopard his spots?"
Jeremiah 13:23a

RACE RELATIONS posed a particularly thorny problem for white southerners at the turn of the century. If the New South prophets were correct and the South would soon become rich, would African Americans share in this heralded prosperity? Would the sweeping socioeconomic changes Richard H. Edmunds and Henry W. Grady predicted open the door for either black social or political equality? If white southerners had their way, the answer, of course, was no.

Southern Baptists faced similar questions in the religious realm. If 1890 to 1920 marked a time when Baptists were experiencing a growing self-awareness that manifested itself in an enlarged view of Baptist social obligation, would blacks stand to benefit?

Superficially, it is tempting to dismiss Southern Baptist involvement in the black community from 1890 to 1920 as meaningless, or, at best, half-hearted. After all, their belief that mountaineers were worthy of assistance resulted in schools for white mountain children. Much like their mountain schools, Southern Baptist orphanages were also white institutions. Yet, there is more than this to Southern Baptist turn-of-the-century racial attitudes.

Between 1890 and 1920, Southern Baptists were vitally interested in racial uplift. White Baptists believed blacks would always be a prominent feature in southern life. They also believed blacks needed salvation and that the gospel offered salvation regardless of one's race.

White Baptists further believed blacks were childlike, needing direction. Consequently, they believed they had an obligation to help blacks find their "place" in southern society.

White Baptists committed themselves to helping blacks build churches for two reasons. Obviously, they believed that churches would advance religious education among blacks. Yet Southern Baptists believed blacks were partially responsible for their own uplift and churches would serve as moral beacons in the black community. Consequently, Southern Baptists eagerly sought black Baptist ministers, especially those who accepted accommodationism, with whom they could work to redeem black souls and bodies. And in the process of uplifting blacks, Baptists reasoned that they were also uplifting themselves.

Joel Williamson has proposed a model that helps put Southern Baptist racial attitudes in perspective. Williamson argues that the post-Reconstruction South saw the reemergence of what he calls an "organic society." This was a society deeply rooted in the idea of "placeness." Regardless of age, sex, or race, everyone had his or her own place within society. Satisfactory social relations, therefore, depended largely upon one's knowing and accepting his or her place. White males were civic and ecclesiastical leaders. At home, they were the heads of their families. Women and children were expected to defer to their authority. As for race, southern white men acted as paternalistic guides to assist blacks in finding their "place."[1]

Williamson also maintains that three dominant racial mentalities permeated southern thinking at the turn of the century. By his definition a mentality is "something less formed than a philosophy . . . [and] something that includes but is more than 'notions,' 'opinions,' and 'attitudes,' all of which suggest vagueness, impermanence, individual thought rather than social thought, and thinking that does not compel action and is very often at variance with behavior."[2] One of these mentalities was the "liberal" mentality. Liberals had noted the progress blacks made during Reconstruction and were duly impressed. They believed that nobody really knew the full potential blacks possessed, and they were willing to "experiment in a search for progress" on behalf of blacks.[3]

Described as "radical," a second mentality reached its zenith between 1889 and 1915. Williamson argues that it was the more pessimistic of the three mentalities and the "most significant for race relations in the twentieth-century South." Radicals believed that because blacks were no longer bound by slavery's constraints, they were reverting to "savagery and bestiality." This "reversion" fostered the rise of what radicals called the "new Negro," who was a threat to white society. Radicals believed "new Negroes" were incorrigible and harbored lust toward white women. Radicals also believed that blacks had no place in the South and that their "disappearance was imminent."[4]

The "conservative" mentality lay somewhere between the other two. Conservatives believed blacks were inherently inferior to whites and would remain so. Contrary to the radicals, however, conservatives believed that blacks were a permanent feature of American life, and their ultimate goal was to help blacks find their place in society. With aid from benevolent whites, they believed blacks could find their niche in southern society, and everyone would live harmoniously. In fact, Williamson notes this attitude extended to both the black and poorer white communities and continues to enjoy a longevity that exceeds either the liberal or radical mentality.[5]

Southern Baptists fit squarely into the conservative mentality. On the one hand, they did not believe that blacks were their social equals. On the other hand, at no time did they articulate a desire to force African Americans from the region. They were perfectly willing, even eager, to accept blacks so long as it was within a paternalistic, white-defined framework. This is perhaps best evidenced by comparing post-Reconstruction black churches with white ideology at the turn of the century.

Churches had always been important in the black community, but they were even more important after the Civil War. Eric Foner argues that blacks formed numerous congregations of their own during Reconstruction because whites refused to recognize them as equals, and they wanted to experience the freedom of running their own religious affairs.[6] These new black churches played a vital role in shaping their respective communities. They served a variety of functions ranging from houses of worship to schools. They also provided a convenient meeting place for social events and various political gatherings. According to Foner, "the church was 'the first social institution fully controlled by blacks in America,' and its multiple functions testified to its centrality in the black community."[7] Logically, ministers quickly became recognized as leading spokesmen in the black community on numerous topics.[8]

Yet newly freed blacks faced numerous problems. Edward L. Wheeler identifies three of these problems in *Uplifting the Race*. Wheeler argues that, first, free blacks scarcely had a concept of what freedom meant. Second, they were not prepared for freedom in that they had neither money, land, nor credit. Third, whites refused to accept blacks as their equals.[9] Wheeler also maintains that black ministers became important spokesmen for the black community, particularly because they championed the "uplift" of African Americans. Wheeler sees uplift as "descriptive of the process by which the freedman was to overcome oppression and achieve the goal of equality."[10] The four basic tenets of uplift were "moral elevation, the improvement of physical conditions, intellectual enlightenment, and spiritual elevation."[11] Moreover, Wheeler indicates that black ministers placed the burden of uplift on blacks themselves rather than whites. Uplift emphasized self-help and self-improvement.[12]

Southern Baptists clearly understood the implications of racial uplift. They had always displayed interest in evangelizing blacks, but white involvement in black affairs could be minimized if blacks would assume responsibility for their own uplift. Moreover, they too saw ministers as the key to uplift. In 1894, one Baptist noted that opportunities existed for religious work among blacks, but the greatest opportunity was in educating black ministers, particularly those whom he called "the choice spirits." Such ministers, he said, were "the ruling spirits of the race." He believed helping black ministers was the most expedient way to help all southern blacks.[13]

Southern Baptists officially began educating blacks in 1894 as a result of the Fortress Monroe Conference. This conference pitted the Home Mission Board (HMB) of the Southern Baptist Convention against the Home Mission Society (HMS) of New York. These rival groups met at Fortress Monroe, Virginia, to determine how they might best pursue their respective missionary objectives.

Trouble between the two organizations had been brewing for some time. In 1882, E. T. Winkler questioned whether the Home Mission Society had the right to work in the South. As president of the Home Mission Board, he upbraided his brethren for aiding Northern Baptists and noted that such cooperation would ultimately undermine all

Southern Baptist Convention work. In assessing this controversy, H. Leon McBeth notes that the ensuing editorial warfare in both Northern and Southern Baptist newspapers was instrumental in alerting Southern Baptists to the "long-range implications of what Winkler called Northern Baptist 'intrusion' in the South."[14]

At that time Henry L. Morehouse was head of the Home Mission Society. Understandably, he was upset by Winkler's remarks and responded by asserting the Society's constitutional and historical precedents for its working throughout the United States, even in the South. He touched a nerve, however, when he suggested that the Home Mission Board had outlived its usefulness and should be disbanded.[15]

In the wake of this controversy Baptists became sensitive to any perceived "wrongdoings" by the Home Mission Society. They did not have to wait long. In 1888, controversy erupted once again. This time, the issue focused on reports to the Home Mission Board from missionaries in Missouri stating that Northern Baptists were soliciting contributions from Southern Baptist churches. After debating the issue, both sides agreed to curtail their proselytizing. Northern missionaries were to confine their solicitations to churches sympathetic to northern organizations, while southern missionaries confined their fundraising to churches sympathetic to southern organizations. Certain churches sent contributions to both agencies, and missionaries in both camps were charged not to disrupt such "amicable arrangements."[16]

It is nearly impossible to determine the extent to which either side took this agreement seriously. One thing is certain: the controversy was still alive in 1889. In April of that year the Home Mission Board drafted a letter to Henry Morehouse. Northerners' canvassing southern churches for contributions was once again an issue. A more serious matter for the Southern Baptists, however, involved cooperative mission work between blacks and whites in Texas. The letter alleged that in 1884 the Home Mission Board and the State Mission Board of Texas had begun to do missionary work with the "colored" Convention of Texas. The letter further alleged that a Rev. Dr. Simmons who was affiliated with the Home Mission Society had convinced the black Baptists of Texas to abandon their joint work with the Home Mission Board and to cast their lot with the Home Mission Society.[17]

Unfortunately, there was no easy solution to these problems. The southern economy was still suffering from the ill effects of the Civil

War. Texas, for example, was divided into five state conventions in the early 1890s, four of which received some funding from the Home Mission Society.[18] Still, Isaac T. Tichenor, secretary of the Home Mission Board, sensed an imminent change. In 1892 he told the Southern Baptist Convention that the Home Board was so active in sending missionaries that "its territory had been reclaimed" and that the Board had won "the confidence of the denomination."[19]

Tichenor was at least half right. The denomination seemed convinced that the Home Board was a worthy organization, but winning the South was another matter. Both missionary agencies continued to make charges and countercharges until 1894, when T. T. Eaton, editor of *The Western Recorder*, suggested that all controversies between the two bodies be settled. Eaton proposed that each body appoint a committee of five to meet and discuss two matters. First, they were to discuss how they might work together among southern blacks. Second, they were to forge a more concrete understanding regarding the territorial limits of both groups with respect to native whites, immigrants, and Indians.[20]

The two committees met at Fortress Monroe, Virginia, on September 12 and 13, 1894. The delegates to this convention agreed not to discuss past issues, but rather to secure mutual cooperation for future mission ventures. By the end of the meeting both sides agreed that since the Home Mission Society had been actively building schools for blacks, control of these schools should remain with the Society. The Southern Baptists would assist these schools by helping to raise funds, recruiting students, and appointing local advisory committees to assist in school administration. Both sides also agreed to cooperate in missionary efforts among blacks, especially in training black ministers and deacons and in the general organization of Negro Baptist missionary work. Finally, the issue of territorial sovereignty was solved when both sides agreed not to solicit funding in areas where missionary work was already established. Instead, they agreed that a more expedient and efficient way to conduct missionary enterprises was to go to areas "not already occupied by the other."[21]

According to McBeth, both sides achieved something substantial. On the one hand, the Home Mission Society received more southern aid for blacks. This in itself was a great victory, but it also reduced the possibility of financial overextension, since the HMS had increased

A School for Black Children, circa 1919. (Courtesy of the Southern Baptist Historical Library and Archives, Historical Commission, SBC, Nashville, Tennessee.)

missionary activities in the west and among immigrants. On the other hand, the Southern Baptists had finally achieved territorial recognition. That is, Southern Baptists would confine their work to the South while their northern brethren would stay north of the Potomac and Ohio rivers.[22]

The Fortress Monroe Conference did not squelch all intersectional bickering, but it did provide the basis for cooperative mission work between the rival agencies. Moreover, it reflects much of the social and cultural tumult that the South experienced in the latter decades of the nineteenth century.

The Home Mission Society would retain control of the schools they had established, but Southern Baptists agreed to assist these existing institutions with advice and limited finances. The net effect of the Fortress Monroe Agreement with respect to black education was that southern and northern Baptists agreed to work together in conjunction with black Baptists to educate black preachers.[23]

The evidence suggests that Southern Baptists subsequently made a sincere attempt to fulfill their obligations. Unfortunately, the results were mixed. In 1898 the Alabama Baptists told the Home Mission Board that they simply could not afford to help pay their portion of missionary expenses in that state. The Committee on Work Among Negroes, a group of Southern Baptists who monitored racial issues, responded by agreeing to pay one fourth of the state's total missionary expenses in the black community provided the Home Mission Society and the state's black Baptists contributed one fourth and one half, respectively. This would leave the Alabama Baptists liable for any remaining missionary debt.[24]

The news from the missionary front, however, was not all bad. While the Alabama Baptists experienced financial difficulty, the North Carolina Baptists reported that the relationship among themselves, the Home Mission Society, and the state's black Baptists was "satisfactory and profitable." Although the minutes do not specify exactly what "satisfactory and profitable" meant, they do indicate that joint work between blacks and whites in North Carolina would continue for at least three more years.[25]

Despite the unevenness of early efforts, the Georgia Baptists agreed upon a plan to educate black ministers in 1899. The plan called for joint cooperation between the Home Mission Society, the Home Mission Board, the Georgia Baptist Convention, and the Negro Baptist Education Society. Their purpose was to meet a perceived need for ministerial training in the black community. Because many black ministers in Georgia had little formal education and no seminary training, this joint body wanted to systemize some type of educational forum that would help offset these deficiencies. They wanted to impress black churches with the importance of Christian education, missions, and stewardship. Finally, they wanted to train young blacks to "make them useful to their race" and encourage the most promising ministers to further their education.[26]

This plan divided Georgia into four districts. A General Educational Missionary would oversee state operations, as well as serve as educational missionary in one of the four districts. The plan also called for a three-year course in theological studies at Atlanta Baptist College, each school year lasting for six months. In addition to the three-year course, each district was to select no fewer than six "central" locations and conduct Bible Schools, or "New Era Institutes." These Institutes would be conducted yearly when the theological course was not in session. They would last from three days to two or more weeks and emphasize "practical instruction" in a variety of subjects designed to help black ministers in church administration and Bible teaching.[27]

By 1900, Southern Baptists were pleased with the progress of their joint venture with blacks and the Home Mission Society. They firmly advocated industrial education for those blacks who were not ministers and privately noted that southern blacks were increasingly interested in their own "development." They also noted that blacks were "revolting from the control of the American Baptist Home Mission Society" and in some cases they were establishing schools of their own.[28]

At the same time, the Home Mission Board said that as blacks were turning away from the Home Mission Society they were turning to white Baptists in the South for aid. This posed a quandary. In light of their agreement with the Home Mission Society regarding joint education work among blacks, what were Southern Baptists to do? There were several problems. Some believed the Home Board was merely spending money to enhance the "power and influence" of the Home Mission Society in the South, yet expenses were a real problem. The Home Mission Society had borne the financial brunt of the "joint venture," and some on the Home Board openly wondered if Southern Baptists would willingly spend more money to educate blacks when denominational colleges and seminaries for whites were struggling.[29]

Establishing bonds that transcended race and culture was not easy. As one scholar has observed, the "New Era" Plan was changed in 1904 into the "Enlarged Plan of Negro Work," largely because of divisions among black Baptists. The "Enlarged Plan" was not significantly different in its objectives from the "New Era" plan. Nevertheless, it limited Southern Baptists to cooperation with the National Baptist Convention, Inc., as the legitimate representative of southern blacks.[30]

In spite of efforts to educate blacks, Southern Baptist involvement in black education was always limited by the assumption that blacks were racially inferior to whites. Antebellum religious leaders devised numerous Biblical justifications for slavery, all of which assumed innate black inferiority. In *Slavery, Segregation and Scripture*, James O. Buswell III identifies five different theories explaining the origins of black people, most of which assume that blackness resulted from a curse God had pronounced upon Noah's son, Ham.[31] Buswell also notes that some did not even bother to justify slavery from scripture; they simply argued that blacks were beasts.[32]

With the end of the Civil War and the ratification of the Thirteenth, Fourteenth, and Fifteenth Amendments to the Constitution, Biblical justifications of slavery were moot. Unfortunately, the same assumptions regarding African-American inferiority lingered stubbornly into the twentieth century, and Baptists were no exception in this regard. In 1911, D. L. Gore, a Baptist layman from Wilmington, North Carolina, wrote, "The race [Negro] is inferior by birth and in every other respect to the white race."[33] Most any white southerner would have said as much in 1911, but Gore quickly added that the root of black inferiority was slavery. "Under these conditions," he said, "it is surprising that there are so many of them that are not only good men and women, but real good citizens."[34]

White racism among turn-of-the-century Southern Baptists is scarcely surprising, but the fact that Gore found blacks to be "good citizens" indicates that, while dedicated to white supremacy, he was not a racial radical. Following Williamson's model, he was rather a racial conservative, and his argument reflected the thought of most Progressive Era Baptists.

The central tenet of Southern Baptist racial conservatism was that blacks were teachable. Gore argued that blacks responded well to responsibility, particularly in agriculture. He advocated giving blacks "a chance" and providing them with education so that they would become "good citizens."[35] He made two things about this education clear. First, he believed blacks needed industrial rather than classical education. He said that blacks were "beginning to find out, like some of the white folk, that the farm is the best place for them."[36] Second, "good citizenship" implied law and order. Gore was suspicious of urban areas, fearing that blacks might fall prey to the town's rabble. He conceded that there were some upstanding African-American citizens in urban areas, but warned that "these town dudes, with their leatherwing trousers on—we do not care to express an opinion on them.

They, however, are imitative and many of them wear the white dude's trousers and hang around the corners as the original wearers did."[37]

C. C. Brown was even more explicit. Brown pastored First Baptist Church, Sumpter, South Carolina, and proposed an "almost radical remedy" to the South's race problem. He believed that black ministers should receive education in "collegiate branches" and the "masses" should receive industrial education. There was one catch: Brown proposed integrated education for black ministers. Taking racial uplift to its logical limit, he believed that blacks needed high "ideals" to which they could aspire. He also believed that blacks could not find such "ideals" among their own people. Consequently, he argued, "The Negro preacher who is to become a genuine benefactor to his race must be educated by Southern white people, and—saints and ministers of grace, defend us!—among Southern white people."[38] Brown admitted that such reasoning was "hard to swallow," but insisted the "Southern white man's burden" was not simply to give money for black education. Rather, southern whites needed to give themselves to this cause, and he challenged Baptists to lead the way.[39]

From a late twentieth-century perspective, Brown's suggestion is not earthshaking. But for 1916, the idea of blacks and whites in the same classroom was a daring suggestion. Moreover, Brown's proposal actually allowed for the formation of a trained, black ministerial elite. Since white southerners would train their preachers, Brown presumably had no fear that they might not preach accommodationism to their congregations. Nevertheless, it is not surprising to note that white Baptists saw themselves as the best moral inspiration the black community could have. Additionally, such a policy was completely within the accepted bounds of "placeness." After all, the masses needed industrial education to equip them for the workplace. But as Brown saw it, uplift began in black pulpits. He said, "The Negro masses will never rise above the Negro preachers and the Negro preachers will never get far above the level of the masses until they acquire the white man's ideals directly from the white man."[40] Whites were to set a moral example for black preachers, who, in turn, were supposed to preach it to their congregations. In this way, Southern Baptists believed they would achieve "uplift" for blacks. Whites were willing to offer some assistance, but clearly, they held blacks partially responsible for their own moral betterment. Presumably, economic advancement would follow.

The concern for black uplift was rooted in white paternalism. Their supposed "inferiority" made blacks appear childlike, needing direction. J. B. Gambrell, editor of the *Baptist Standard*, said, "They must walk on their own feet and it is for us to steady their steps and lead them on till they are sufficient in themselves."[41] The same author said that blacks were "clay" and whites were in a position to be "potters." Whites should, therefore, be careful how they shaped their vessels. He warned, "We can mar the vessel or we can shape it for service and glory."[42] Clearly, to be a "fitting vessel" in the black community was equivalent to accepting an inferior place to whites on the emerging socioeconomic ladder.

Inherent within the white paternalistic scheme was the sincere belief that whites "owed" blacks some degree of uplift. They conceded that blacks had immortal souls for whom Christ had died. Hence, they saw the primary thrust of their work among blacks as religious, and they approached their task as missionaries. An editorial in *The Home Field* noted, "The Negro problem is a religious problem rather than a political or social problem."[43] It was no accident, then, that at Fortress Monroe, Southern Baptists chose to assist blacks in building churches while the Home Mission Society supported black schools. Southern Baptists believed that by equipping black ministers and building black churches, they could provide a value structure for blacks that would prevent them from falling into debauchery. In this manner, blacks would be helping themselves.

There was also a highly self-serving aspect to racial uplift. Those whites who chose to comment on race relations tended to see the southern black experience intertwined with that of southern whites. They believed that by uplifting blacks they were uplifting whites in the process. Gambrell noted that the South's ten million blacks were a tremendous industrial force hamstrung by "ignorance and immorality." Blacks constituted the very "mud-sill" of the South's industrial system. They needed evangelism, and more. He asserted, "We must evangelize and teach the Negroes for their sakes and ours. The spirit that would save them will save us."[44]

This idea of mutual "salvation" was somewhat naive. Whites believed that immorality in the black community was due largely to whites who furnished them with gambling facilities and liquor. They believed if they could lift blacks out of such circumstances, they would also uplift whites who were "lowering" themselves in pandering to such vices in black communities.[45]

Baptists also saw something of a challenge in uplifting blacks. B. F. Riley, a Baptist minister and head of The Southern Negro Anti-Saloon Federation, stated the case plainly when he noted that whites were eager to evangelize white foreigners from whom they had received nothing. Therefore, it was inconsistent not to evangelize and assist blacks, whom he described as "faithful" during the South's darkest days. He chided would-be detractors by noting that anyone who argued that blacks were beyond hope were casting aspersions on white ability to Christianize them, as well as on the gospel itself. Additionally, Riley argued that Baptists, indeed all southerners, should be grateful for the "Negro" presence in the region. If nothing else, blacks had discouraged immigrants from learning to whistle Dixie. "After the last word about the Negro has been said," he observed, "the fact remains that but for his presence in the South we should have had, as a servant class, the refuse and the riff-raff from southern and eastern Europe. Instead of the tractable and docile Negroes, a people who are known and who know us, we should have had the maffia [sic], the black-hand, the skeptic and infidel, and the irreligious, and criminal class already alluded to, schooled in centuries of vice and crime."[46]

In analyzing white Southern Baptist sentiment toward blacks, it is immediately apparent that the Baptists never saw their involvement in the black community as a means to social equality. C. C. Brown, the man who advocated integrated ministerial classrooms, prefaced his "bold" declaration by saying, "my remedy is almost radical, and comes near arousing my own sense of disgust."[47] To assure readers that his credentials as a white supremacist were still intact, he quickly added that, "The nightmare of social equality—a something of which I am not able to divest myself—disturbs all the best dreams of my life. It is not a law of caste, but a law of nature."[48] He closed by asserting that, "The Southern man will never come to believe that the Negro is just as good as he is, and the only difference is the color of the skin. We who live among them—and they themselves—know this is not true. It would never occur to us to teach such heresy. Our doctrine would be better, and based upon the truth."[49] For Brown, the "truth" was that blacks were innately inferior to whites, and to teach anything less was absurd.

This was not an isolated view among Southern Baptists. Weston Bruner, the Home Mission Board's Superintendent of Evangelism, told a correspondent to *The Home Field* that blacks constituted the "greatest field of service" for Southern Baptists. He also expressed disgust for what he believed was paltry support to evangelize blacks. As for social equality, he believed there were only two problems—whites and blacks. "As we have a fuller understanding of each other," he said, "each will understand his place the better and Negro leaders themselves as they come in touch with us understand that social equality is out of the question."[50] Moreover, he added, "social equality in the Southland can never be except where all moral standards and ideals are eliminated. Where these are first, social equality is furthest away."[51]

Some black religious leaders may have accepted this limited assistance and white supremacist rhetoric because they believed they had no other options. E. C. Morris, President of the National Baptist Convention, noted that he read with interest anything that white men had to say about southern blacks. He praised Baptist leaders such as C. C. Brown and J. B. Gambrell as defenders of the status quo. Morris observed that in their denominational capacities these men spoke often with black leaders and, "I venture to say that not a single one of them can point to an instance where any black man has ever intimated that there was a desire for the social intermingling of the races."[52] Morris also agreed that blacks and whites shared the same interests, particularly in economic terms, and it was ultimately in the best interest of white people to educate blacks. Here again, though, he agreed that such education should be primarily religious.[53]

The emphasis whites placed on religious education provides a second key in analyzing Southern Baptist attitudes toward blacks. Whites took black religious work seriously. At one level, they believed blacks needed salvation as much as whites did. In fact, they believed whites owed blacks the gospel, and they noted the irony of sending money to evangelize Africans while millions of southern blacks received little attention.[54]

Southern Baptists had little problem accepting blacks on an equal spiritual basis. Accepting blacks on an equal social basis, however, was a different matter. Yet, religion still played a prominent role in shaping

Southern Baptist views on race relations. Their entire philosophy of uplifting the Negro race was rooted in their paternalistic religious assumptions. They simply could not divorce themselves from the notion that southern blacks needed them as positive role models. Baptists believed that if they could instill a "moral code" within blacks, they would advance the race. This moral code would curb gambling, drinking, and the like, and would also provide blacks with the same religious assumptions whites had. Blacks would accept Jesus Christ as the Savior from sin's consequences; blacks would also become involved in their own local churches staffed by white-trained ministers. Meanwhile, white Southern Baptists would set a good moral example for blacks to emulate.

This framework fits Williamson's model of turn-of-the-century racial attitudes. By assuming their self-appointed "place" as the South's superior race, whites, particularly most Southern Baptists, believed it was their duty to assist blacks in finding *their* place in southern society. They were not radicals who wanted to rid the South of African Americans. Quite the contrary. They believed blacks would forever be a prominent feature of southern life. But since they assumed blacks were inferior, many Southern Baptists wanted to lead blacks into a white-defined socioeconomic role. Additionally, Southern Baptist involvement in the black community was based on the same religious assumption that precipitated Social Christianity among the whites: that the best way to effect social change was first by individual conversion. Just as Baptist leaders believed white mountaineers needed religion to help them meet the challenge of their "coming" wealth, Baptists also saw individual conversion as the first step in uplifting blacks. Unlike white mountaineers, full social equality was beyond the black community's immediate reach. Nevertheless, upon obtaining salvation, blacks could then learn their "place" through white example and black church leadership. Whites would help blacks find their place by recruiting and training a black ministerial elite that would, in turn, preach accommodationism to their congregations.

Finding likeminded allies among African-American ministers was relatively simple. August Meier argues that regardless of denomination, the majority of turn-of-the-century black ministers endorsed accommodationism as the most legitimate means of addressing socioeconomic problems among African Americans.[55] Southern Baptists ultimately found a ready spokesman in Richard Carroll. Born in Barn-well County, South Carolina, around 1860, Carroll rose to prominence between 1890 and 1920. Unfortunately, the biographical information on this man is sketchy. He was recognized as a preacher, but there is no indication that he ever pastored a specific church. On one occasion Carroll quipped, "I'm not fit to be a pastor because I don't want any-body to pay me who does not like me."[56]

Initially, Carroll won respect among whites for his work with black children. An unnamed benefactor gave Carroll a parcel of land near Columbia, South Carolina, where he built a home to accommodate African-American orphans and delinquents. Resident children grew as much of their food as they could, and Carroll paid remaining expenses from voluntary contributions he received from his speaking engage-ments.[57]

It is also perhaps ironic that Carroll became a celebrity among whites; Richard Carroll was half white. On one occasion he said, "I'm not a nigger and I'm not a white man. . . . My mother said I am the son of a high class white aristocrat and have got good blood in me. I don't know; she never would tell me who my father was."[58]

Given white radical attitudes about miscegenation, Carroll could well have been scorned, but he was not. Rather, white Southern Bap-tists respected him, and the reasons are simple. Southern Baptists were not racial radicals. They believed blacks had a "place" in southern so-ciety, and they were determined to fit them into that place. More im-portant, Carroll was the kind of black leader white Southern Baptists could best use to their own advantage. For example, he claimed his mother was a slave, yet he attained prominence and recognition in both the black and white communities. Southern Baptists capitalized on Carroll's image, which they perceived as the perfect illustration of what initiative, hard work, and accepting "one's place" could accom-plish. In short, Carroll appealed to Southern Baptists because he ac-cepted their assumptions regarding southern race relations.

The central white conservative assumption regarding blacks was ra-cial inferiority, and Carroll echoed this assumption. When he spoke on race, his pulpit oratory did not differ significantly from that of white Baptist leaders. "The Anglo-Saxon race is unquestionably the leading race on earth," he said on one occasion. "God has entrusted to it in-fluence, power, dominion and not least, the Bible."[59] Carroll's reference to the Bible is significant because he was suggesting that whites had a responsibility to propagate Christianity. This obligation extended into the black community as well. Hence, Carroll, much like antebellum apologists, maintained that slavery had been a "positive good" for blacks. He argued that slavery had actually benefited the Kingdom of God by bringing blacks into the presence of whites on the North American continent. Whites, he said, needed "the Negro's splendid muscles and brawn" for civilization's advancement. Blacks benefited by learning about the white man's God, not to mention the discipline of hard labor. In Carroll's mind it was scarcely an even trade. He noted, "As the Negro's needs were greater and more numerous, he received greater benefit from the system of American slavery than did the white man."[60]

To further allay white suspicions, Carroll maintained that blacks posed no threat to white supremacy. He noted that blacks were characteristically "gentle and docile." During the Civil War, blacks remained loyal and harbored no animosity toward their masters and mistresses. Even in death, "When bleeding and wounded the master fell, the devoted Negro bore him tenderly home to die and at his burial shed tears of sincere regret at his grave."[61]

Carroll's racial assumptions and accommodation extended even to his eschatology. While the United States prepared for war in Europe, Carroll predicted the world's end was near. Yet, the real problem, as Carroll saw it, was the Orient, not Europe. He believed that the "yellow races," especially Japan and China, would wage war against the United States. At this cataclysmic time the white people would call upon blacks to help them win this war.[62]

Carroll also had a way of ingratiating himself with white Baptists by criticizing fellow black ministers in matters where they conducted themselves differently from whites. Differing pulpit oratory styles was one such object of Carroll's scorn. He chided his fellow blacks for their sing-song cadence, accusing them of believing that their ability to "moan" was more important than their message's content. He also noted that at one time whites had preached in a similar fashion, but later preachers "rose above it." He believed black preachers should do likewise. He asked, "Why cannot Negro preachers take the same consideration and put down this whang-doodling?"[63]

In the same article, Carroll criticized northern blacks for their positions regarding race relations. Southern blacks, in his estimate, needed no "federal interference." Bringing blacks into political prominence would simply place them "in an awkward situation." Moreover, Jim Crow laws and lynching were matters that in his opinion were best left untouched.[64] The editors of *The Home Field* praised Carroll as a "courageous leader of his people," and they extended him "and the large and increasing number of Negro leaders of his character [their] sincere esteem and brotherly regard."[65]

It is nearly impossible to distinguish Richard Carroll's pulpit rhetoric from his genuine feelings. One thing, though, is beyond dispute: Carroll clearly understood southern political reality. He knew that white race-baiters pitted black interests against white interests in order to get white votes. On more than one occasion he lamented the fact that blacks were leaving the South. Nevertheless, he understood that they sought opportunity and justice. He cautiously advocated protection of black property, better schools, and higher wages. But even when he criticized southern society, he took great care not to be too critical. He said, "Let the white politicians in discussing issues leave the Negro out and no longer ride the Negro into office. It has been proved that these white men who abuse Negroes are just as good to them in their hearts as other white men. But they can only get into office by abusing the Negro to a certain class of white men who will only give their vote to the man who will promise to work against the Negro."[66]

While it is true that Carroll may have wanted to curb violence against blacks by not attacking white racism directly, it is also true that he had a paternalistic attitude toward his own race. He feared that in leaving the South for northern industrial centers, blacks were opening a Pandora's box of cultural woes. He argued that blacks were better suited to the South, particularly because southerners were more indulgent than northerners. He further criticized blacks for a perceived lack of industry that had stigmatized them as an unreliable component in the work force. He complained, "They [blacks] work one day and loaf two days: they work one week and stay off a week. They waste time attending funerals, going on picnics and excursions. These habits they cannot carry into the North and keep employed."[67] Carroll also believed that such idleness would lead to confrontations with authorities. When warranted, he urged northern cities to "free the city of undesirable negroes from the South. Send them back to us. We can take care of them."[68]

Carroll had a clear idea how to address southern racial woes. He believed that whites should help blacks receive an education whereby they might attain their rightful "place" in society. His argument rested on two assumptions. Much like his white counterparts, Carroll argued that whites could not impede black socioeconomic progress without impeding their own. Education was good, therefore, for both the black and white communities. Carroll also believed whites owed a debt to blacks. This debt was not monetary; rather, it was the help necessary for blacks to find their way in the world.

In defining black "placeness," Carroll argued that blacks belonged on the farm. In 1917, World War I had placed new demands on the agricultural sector. Carroll believed that blacks were missing a good opportunity to farm by seeking jobs in northern war industries. At one level, he believed that most blacks had no skill that would be beneficial to northern industry in the first place. Since most blacks came from rural backgrounds, farming was better suited to their abilities.[69]

At another level, however, Carroll was suspicious of blacks and wealth. He noted that some had urged blacks to acquire wealth as a means of solving the "race problem." He scoffed at such notions and reminded fellow blacks that riches were fleeting. He believed it was far more important to acquire character, an attribute that was guaranteed to remain after fortunes were spent. He said, "Christianity is shown in our lives, the inner life must overcome the outer life and our bodies under subjection and we must abide by the teachings of Jesus Christ."[70] Such men of character were most likely to produce "love, mercy, kindness, politeness and peace."[71] Clearly, Richard Carroll believed that these attributes, properly used, would earn respect for blacks in the white community and be the appropriate docile attitude for a dependent people.

The education Carroll advocated for blacks had religious overtones. He made this clear on numerous occasions. In May 1915, the Southern Baptist Convention met in Houston, Texas. Carroll addressed the messengers on the subject, "The South's Debt to the Negro." He praised blacks for their docility and faithfulness but called on Southern Baptists for help. He quoted St. Paul's words to the Romans, "I am debtor both to the Greeks and to the Barbarians, to the wise and the un-wise."[72] He further noted, "Ignorance is a crime," and he said that blacks deserved to receive an education, work for a livelihood, and en-joy equal protection under the law. He also noted that blacks deserved the gospel. He believed the gospel saved individuals from sin, but in the process of conversion and the ensuing spirit of brotherhood and goodwill, the gospel created other implications. In his words, "It settles all race problems. It makes us recognize man as our brothers and God as our Father. It makes us do good unto all men as I have opportunity."[73]

Carroll's thinking is clear and does not differ from that of many white Baptist leaders. Christian conversion was supposed to produce fundamental changes within one's disposition. This newfound love and respect for others was then supposed to create concern for the less fortunate and this, in turn, led to Social Christianity. There was a twist. Carroll believed white assistance was only a temporary mea-sure. He believed blacks were willing to be subservient to whites, but he noted, "With all of our educated men and great leaders and numer-ous organizations, we are not yet prepared to go alone. We are yet in our childhood. We spend much time in play. The spirit of jealousy is rampant. We need to cooperate in Christian work."[74]

White southerners delighted in Carroll's rhetoric. He extolled the virtues of Anglo-Saxon superiority. He was careful not to criticize the existing order. And he did not ask whites to provide blacks with more than they were prepared to give already. One correspondent for the *Aiken Journal and Review* said it best when he praised Carroll's efforts to "reconcile the two races of the South, without awakening social conflict."[75] Baptist presses likewise praised Carroll as a man of "un-usual gifts with an amiable and attractive personality."[76]

Perhaps the most succinct statement of Carroll's appeal came after his death in 1929. Victor Masters, Superintendent of Publicity for The Home Mission Board, wrote a lengthy eulogy in which he proudly called Carroll a friend. Masters praised Carroll for his moderation, es-pecially on racial issues. He noted that unlike others, even some whites, Carroll was no racial instigator. "Richard Carroll," he said, "deliberately and firmly refused to take up with any of those mis-guided ideas that have been fostered by some of his own race leaders, to the effect that Negroes must place a chip on their shoulders and demand 'the rights' of the white man."[77] Moreover, Masters said Carroll carefully avoided overfamiliarity with white women, unguarded speech toward white men, and was content to "let sleeping taboos lie." He impressed Masters as the type of man who wanted to effect social change from within, as did most Southern Baptists. For Carroll, this meant "putting it on the consciences of Southern Whites that they should treat the blacks about them or in their service with equity and kindness and consideration."[78] Masters believed that nothing short of black accommodation would settle the "race question" in the South, and he praised Carroll for his efforts in this area. "He was less well-known than Booker T. Washington perhaps as a statesman," said Masters, "but his heart grasped the root of the matter and with great charm and persuasiveness he wrought at it—never discouraged though there was plenty to discourage."[79]

It is scarcely surprising that Southern Baptists adopted the attitudes they did. Some had been slave owners, and they doubtless found the notion of social equality with their former chattel to be most distasteful. Even William Louis Poteat, one of the more progressive Baptists of the early twentieth century, fondly recalled growing up with Nat, his slave companion. "My father gave him to me for my own," Poteat recalled, "and in a way I belonged to him. And wheresoever Louis went, why Nat was sure to go."

> Except he did not follow me to school,
> For that was clear against the rule;
> But with a native, untaught skill,
> He wrote his name where it brightens still.[80]

The problem for Southern Baptists was that they could not move beyond their old racial assumptions.

Yet it is too cynical to suggest that white Southern Baptists were merely content to revel in their racism. As they sought to uplift blacks, Baptists consistently displayed genuine concern for blacks as individuals. They believed blacks had souls worthy of salvation, and many championed "home missions" among black Americans over "foreign missions" to black Africans. Additionally, by first addressing the sin problem within individuals, Southern Baptists, perhaps unwittingly, applied the same assumption to blacks as they did whites: Real change began with individual conversion. Once individuals were converted, they could begin to initiate moral reformation within their communities.

Neither should it surprise anyone that Baptists sought to work through black ministers. Southern Baptists wanted blacks, as much as possible, to be responsible for their own "uplift." This thinking is perfectly consistent with the particular movement culture that reinforced Southern Baptist polity at the turn of the century. This movement culture stressed self-help, democracy, and stability. By effecting uplift through black churches, African Americans helped themselves. True, most blacks were disfranchised by 1910, but whites argued that blacks were not ready to participate in the political process. They first needed to assume their proper place. Once this was accomplished, the South would have order—and, most assumed, prosperity.

Nevertheless, by preaching accommodationism white Baptists faced several ironies. Nearly all Southern Baptists believed that something should be done for blacks, but the same compassion that sparked this concern also limited what Baptists could, or would, do. They consistently scoffed at classical education for blacks, and they did practically nothing to ensure their social equality. At the same time, Southern Baptists engaged in uplifting blacks in fulfillment of what they perceived as a moral duty. Indeed, Southern Baptists preached racial self-help and uplift, but to what end? The gospel message of salvation in Jesus Christ emphatically demanded that whites evangelize the black community. Nonetheless, the Baptist vision of uplift never implied political aims for blacks, and their social aims were never well defined. If uplift brought meaningful change to the black community, a reduction in crime, or an increase in one's personal living standard, well and good. If not, most Baptists were not going to press the issue. They still wanted black people to occupy the lowest rungs of the South's social and economic ladders. In the process, Southern Baptist missiology became a means—either explicitly or implicitly—of keeping black people in their place.

Perhaps the supreme irony lies in the philosophy of "uplift" and accommodation. As Edward L. Wheeler points out in *Uplifting the Race*, the concept of "uplift" admitted that blacks indeed had potential of some type.[81] It was no quantum leap of reasoning for black people to see that if ministers could be standard-bearers, others could too. Almost prophetically, B. F. Riley, a white Southern Baptist champion of social uplift, noted in 1910, "While we may now neglect and despise the Negro, it may be to our future sorrow. He is now ready and responsive. He can be won. We have talked and written much about the Negro; the time has come for action."[82] Baptist "action" in this regard was paternalistic and designed to keep blacks in a subservient position whereby they would continue as little more than "hewers of wood and drawers of water." Every positive step forward for blacks, regardless of how small, helped erode the false assumption of black inferiority, and Riley was doubtless correct: blacks would accept whatever aid they could receive. He also correctly noted that Baptists had "talked and written much" about race relations. Regrettably, they never reached the heights of their lofty rhetoric.

7

REASSESSING A LEGACY
Southern Baptists, Social Christianity,
and Regional Context

"Let us hear the conclusion of the whole matter . . . "
Ecclesiastes 12:13a

B<small>ETWEEN</small> 1890 <small>AND</small> 1920, Southern Baptists displayed increasing awareness and involvement in societal problems. In 1913, they established The Social Service Commission to highlight specifically "the Christian's responsibility in social relations with special reference to marriage and the family, crime and juvenile delinquency, industrial relations, race relations, beverage alcohol, Christian citizenship, and such other problems relating to social morality that may confront the Christian conscience."[1] During its early years this agency primarily attacked alcohol and its ill effects on society. In 1953, the Social Service Commission was renamed The Christian Life Commission, and its scope was broadened to address such problems as divorce, gambling, crime, and the impact of movies on society.[2]

Establishing The Social Service Commission, however, did not mean that Baptists had abandoned preexisting institutions such as orphanages. Baptists were proud of their childcare facilities in 1920, and they would remain regular features of Baptist life throughout the twentieth century. Mountain schools, however, were not as fortunate, and by the end of 1931 Baptists no longer supported schools for mountain children. By 1930, the South's state governments were expanding public education into mountainous regions. State-sponsored schools quickly supplanted many religious schools largely because state conventions began decreasing appropriations for mountain schools. Quite simply, they could neither afford them nor justify the duplication once state governments began to spend more money on education. On a less savory level, mountain school work ceased because C. S. Carnes, Treasurer of The Home Mission Board from 1919 to 1928, embezzled over $900,000 in Baptist funds. He confessed in 1928, but Baptists were unable to recover completely their misappropriated funds. Thus, the Great Depression hit Baptists particularly hard. They were forced to cut financial corners, and since states were spending more for public schools, the mountain schools became expendable.[3]

In spite of what Southern Baptists accomplished through social ministry, some remain unconvinced that southern evangelicals participated extensively in Social Christianity. Samuel S. Hill, Jr., has detected a leading characteristic of southern religious groups to be their "ethos without ethic" in terms of social awareness and action. By this, he means that southern religious groups have traditionally tended to reinforce existing cultural folkways without offering meaningful social criticism. "The church in the South has not seen responsibility for the society as its primary task," Hill argues, "yet it has been inordinately responsive to its societal-cultural framework."[4]

This suggested dichotomy between northern and southern churches is not just false; it focuses on extremes. Some see southern churches as theologically conservative entities interested only in individual conversion, whereas they view northern churches as more theologically liberal with a more proactive role in shaping society. Making this assumption conveniently ignores northern religious conservatism, as well as strong sentiment against the Social Gospel among northern churches. It also suggests that conversionism could neither initiate positive social change nor meet personal, "non-spiritual" human needs.

Yet Hill's observation begs the question, How should one assess the Southern Baptist legacy of Social Christianity? To what extent did Baptists really want to change society? Did their emphasis on missions and evangelism make turn-of-the-century Baptists reformers?

Perhaps the most fruitful context for answering these questions lies in one of the more innovative works to date on southern religious history. In 1980, Charles Reagan Wilson's *Baptized in Blood—The Religion of the Lost Cause, 1865–1920*, provided new insights into the southern evangelical mind. Basing his study on standard, primary material, and on the theoretical work of sociologist Robert N. Bellah and anthropologists Clifford Geertz and Anthony F. C. Wallace, Wilson argued that defeat in the Civil War forced southerners to forge a new collective identity for themselves. Southern ministers developed a distinct southern civil religion by fusing "Lost Causism" (the notion that southern culture was superior to northern culture despite the South's defeat) with evangelical Christianity.[5]

By exploring the cultural and intellectual implications of the New South's developing civil religion, Wilson concluded that southern ministers viewed the emerging modern world with ambivalence, and that they self-consciously sought to fashion the New South with an eye to the Old South's best cultural values. Their "new" world would cherish gallantry and loyalty. It would likewise be pure and virtuous. Inherently conservative, this "new" order would dedicate itself to preserving the cultural status quo, but it would simultaneously display an uncanny ability to adapt itself to the South's changing socioeconomic environment.[6]

While Wilson's work skillfully traces the cultural and intellectual contours of this new civil religion, my own work has sought to explore how one group, the Southern Baptists, expressed their social concerns at the turn of the century. If southern evangelicals, particularly Baptists, emphasized personal conversion, could they participate meaningfully in Social Christianity? I have argued that they could—and did. Much as Dewey W. Grantham has identified a well-defined set of needs that produced a distinctively southern Progressive Movement, so also southern religious groups addressed their social problems in a way that reflected their commitment to maintaining a conservative, albeit more humane, regime within their regional context.[7]

Between 1890 and 1920, Southern Baptists exhibited a distinct, identifiable tendency to address a broad spectrum of social concerns. Conversionism was central, indeed pivotal, in providing them with a platform from which they could address society's problems. Southern Baptists demonstrated their social ethos and ethic as they synthesized evangelism and social ministry to create what this work has called Social Christianity. On the one hand, they believed they were God's ambassadors of evangelism. In keeping with what they understood to be their spiritual mission, their ethos, briefly stated, was reflected in Matthew 28:19-20:

Go ye therefore, and teach all nations, baptizing them in the name of the Father, and of the Son, and of the Holy Ghost: Teaching them to observe all things whatsoever I have commanded you: and, lo, I am with you always, even unto the end of the world. Amen.

On the other hand, their ethic was equally simple: Better people make better societies. This ethic was well suited to the South's new "Lost Cause"-oriented society, which valued personal virtue and social order. As a result, Southern Baptist mission work was intended to accomplish two goals rather than one. Preaching Christ's gospel prepared souls for God's kingdom. Before going to heaven, however, ministers' flocks were expected to behave themselves in a manner consistent with their heavenly calling.

Between 1890 and 1920, Southern Baptists addressed contemporary social problems within a distinctly southern cultural context. Their particular worldview rested upon several basic assumptions. Southerners emphasized the family and the church as society's most fundamental institutions. They also valued community. Joel Williamson has identified the turn-of-the-century South as an "organic society" where everyone must find his or her "place." Hence, one's family, church affiliation, and home community were important to southern self-identification. Moreover, by addressing societal ills through churches and such social networks as families and communities, southerners, especially Baptists, may have camouflaged their Social Christianity to later generations with differing cultural assumptions.

The extent to which Baptists may be deemed reformers, then, depends largely on how one defines reform. If a reformer is one who seeks radical or immediate change and stands willing to use the state's power to enact change, the answer is no, Baptists were not reformers in the traditional Progressive Era sense.[8] But there is more to reform than radicalism and cries for social legislation. Scholars who emphasize the "salvationist model" and who see southern evangelicals as interested only in spiritual matters miss a much broader point. Southern Baptists believed that social problems such as crime, violence, theft, and vice threatened community stability and family order. They also believed that such problems were curable, but not through legislative mandate.

Individual conversion was merely the first step in initiating reform. Southern Baptists believed that only if one stood in the proper relationship with God could one stand in a truly proper relationship with other people. Achieving the proper relationship with God, they believed, was possible only through conversion to Christianity. The Christian's subsequent "walk of faith" involved applying Christian ethics such as self-sacrifice, mutual respect, and brotherly love to all social relationships. Stated another way, Baptists believed that the only way to build a better society was to make better people or, more specifically, for God to make better people through conversion. They avoided calling for legislative changes to alter social behavior because they believed these changes produced superficial results. Between 1890 and 1920, Southern Baptists believed that Christians living Christlike lives would exert a positive influence on existing social structures and alter them to provide the greatest benefit to all members of society. Hence, Baptists were reformers of a sort, but they were "passive reformers," believing that conversion and one's faith would naturally produce desirable social change.

Yet Southern Baptists were neither content to live with their social status quo nor allow their culture to imprison them. They were, rather, actively involved in shaping their culture. They wanted to take what they saw as the best of regional culture, christianize it, and forge a new world, or region, framed by religious assumptions with deep family and community roots. With this emphasis on family and self-conscious identity with the antebellum world, it is not surprising to find a strong current of paternalism in Southern Baptist social ministries. Most southern churchmen at the turn of the century had fought for the Confederacy in the War Between the States. As the South looked to a new century, they doubtless saw themselves not only as the most fit to lead but also as possessing a mandate to mold the South according to "godly dictates."

The relationship between individual conversion and the "organic society" is readily apparent in the numerous social ministries Southern Baptists established between 1890 and 1920. They built orphanages because parentless children needed assistance. Baptists also found a specific Biblical mandate to relieve "the fatherless."[9] Yet Baptist orphanages sought to provide far more than mere relief for orphans. Each facility tried to furnish its charges with a homelike environment, as well as education and health care. As surrogate "families," Southern Baptist orphanages sought to equip children for their adult lives in a manner, given their limitations, not unlike a natural family. In turn, they believed this familylike environment would help each child find her or his place in society.

Perhaps more than the orphanages, Southern Baptist mountain schools reflect a certain paternalistic understanding of mountaineers. They likewise demonstrate the Southern Baptist commitment to evangelization and societal change through individual conversion. The Baptists found no Biblical mandate to build schools, but they wanted to prepare mountaineers for the prosperity that some believed was imminent. They also used such schools to develop a sense of pride within the community. Additionally, each mountain school the Southern Baptists supported taught Bible classes. They were convinced that, apart from the gospel of Christ, there would be no religious or social uplift for mountaineers.

Even in racial issues Baptists remained committed to their basic premise that conversion should be the first step on the road to a new society. Southern Baptists believed that blacks needed social and economic uplift. Regrettably, Baptists were not immune to the racist assumptions that permeated much of white society at the turn of the century. Consequently, white Southern Baptists believed blacks were inferior to whites and prescribed little that would uplift blacks socially or economically. Southern Baptists were unclear exactly where the African-American "place" was in the organic society, but one thing was certain: They believed it was a place below whites. Left on their own, black southerners had to pull themselves up by their own bootstraps.

Religious uplift was a different matter. Southern Baptists felt obligated to help blacks in spiritual matters, especially church building and educating black ministers. Believing that the most effective ministry for the black community came from black ministers, white Southern Baptists enlisted black ministers and trained them to point others to Christ. They lauded black leaders like Richard Carroll with whom they agreed, and they ignored those with whom they disagreed. They also believed the same gospel that benefited whites with a new social outlook benefited blacks as well.

Those who see southern evangelicals as having no social awareness sometimes note that southerners failed to develop a social critique and therefore became accomplices to the South's socioeconomic elite.[10] Again, such criticism misses a broader picture. It is true that turn-of-the-century Southern Baptists developed neither a critique of capitalism nor industrialization. But then, the most recent scholarship suggests that even ardent Social Gospelers in the north experienced difficulty in sustaining their critiques of society.[11] Southern Baptists believed humanity's problems stemmed from sin rather than industrialization. Theirs was a critique of the soul's condition, but it was one's sinfulness, they believed, that led to other social problems such as theft, drunkenness, and abandonment.

By conceptualizing society's problems as the result of sin in the abstract, Southern Baptists found it easier to attack specific manifestations of sinful behavior than to criticize society at large. When they did offer critical observations, their "critique" tended to be piecemeal and highly selective. The result was that Baptists responded to a series of important, well-defined issues that needed immediate attention. Even then, they stuck closely to their commitment to win souls, and they found that they could justify their social endeavors by linking them to evangelism.

It is true that Southern Baptists emphasized individual conversion, but to argue that they displayed no concern for society at large misses the point. Baptist success or failure to address social problems between 1890 and 1920 should be analyzed according to contemporary social mores and not late twentieth-century standards. Unlike certain antebellum reformers, Southern Baptists were not driven by millennialistic assumptions.[12] Given the fact that Southern Baptists believed the only route to a new, better world began with conversion, it is not surprising that they built institutions that reflected a commitment to the family and community.

One could rightly argue that this worldview, which emphasized personal conversion and application of Christian ethics, was naive. After all, Christians do not always operate from purest motives. Yet this criticism also misses the point. The real question is, How successfully did Baptists translate their rhetoric into reality? In many ways this question is open for more discussion. This work has argued that given their cultural climate and ideological assumptions, Baptists successfully translated their social concern into social ministry. They sought to find a "place" for whites and blacks alike. Moreover, they cast themselves as champions of commonfolk. It was a paternalistic, often condescending concern. Regarding blacks, it was steeped in racism and white supremacy. Nonetheless, it called for education and, to a lesser extent, social justice through law and order and the notion of one's "place" in society.

APPENDIX I*

Southern Baptist Mountain Mission Schools

School	Established	HMB Aid Begun	HMB Aid Discontinued
North Carolina:			
Fruitland Institute	1889	1900	1930
Mars Hill College	1857	1900	1928
Mountain View Institute	1912	1912	1929
Alexander Schools, Inc.	1900	1902	1929
Murphy Institute	1903	1903	1915
Mitchell Institute	1903	1903	1923
Haywood Institute	1893	1900	1927
Yancey Collegiate Institute	1900	1907	1926
Liberty Piedmont Institute	?	Aid for a brief time	
Mountain Park Institute	?	Aid for a brief time	
South Carolina:			
North Greenville Academy	1893	1905	1929
Six Mile Academy	1912	1912	1928
Sparton Academy	1905	1905	1922
Long Creek Academy	1913	1913	1922

* This chart is reproduced from the *Encyclopedia of Southern Baptists* (ESB), vol. 2, © copyright 1958. Renewed 1986 Broadman Press. All rights reserved. Used by permission.

Appendix I

School	Established	HMB Aid Begun	HMB Aid Discontinued
Virginia:			
Lee Baptist Institute	1903	1909	1929
Oak Hill Academy	1911	1911	1922
Alabama:			
Eldridge Academy	1906	1906	1931
Beeson Academy	1908	1908	1921
Gaylesville Academy	1906	1906	1923
Tennessee River Institute	1907	1907	1927
Kentucky:			
Magoffin Institute	1904	1904	1931
Hazard Baptist Institute	1905	1905	1931
Barbourville Baptist Institute	1905	1905	1931
Cumberland College	HMB assisted for a brief period		
Oneida Institute	1899	1902	1903
Georgia:			
Hiawassee Academy	1887	1891	1930
Blairsville Collegiate Institute	1905	1911	1929
Bleckley Memorial Institute	1913	1913	1924
Draketown Institute	1912	1913	1917
North Georgia Baptist Institute	1900	1902	1925

School	Established	HMB Aid Begun	HMB Aid Discontinued
Tennessee:			
Harrison-Chilhowee Institute	1881	1904	1929
Smoky Mountain Academy	?	1920	1929
Cosby Academy	1914	1914	1924
Watauga Academy	1882	1906	1931
Doyle College	1884	1905	1927
Andersonville Institute	1907	1907	1918
Stoctons Valley Academy	1911	1912	1928
Unaka Academy	1911	1912	1915
Carson-Newman College	HMB aided in support of a Bible teacher for a number of years.		
Arkansas:			
Mountain Home College	1890	1916	1929
Armo Baptist Academy	1918	1918	1929
Newton County Academy	1920	1920	1929
Maynard Academy	1916	1916	1927
Hagarville Academy	1919	1919	1927
Missouri:			
Southwest Baptist College	1878	1918	1929

APPENDIX II*

Report of Committee on
Work Among the Negroes

November 3, 1899.

Your Committee on Work among the Negroes respectfully submits the following report:

1. At the regular meeting of the Board on Tuesday, October the 8th, a communication from Dr. McVicar, suggesting some amendments to the Articles of Co-operation for Georgia was referred to this Committee with power to act. Action of your Committee upon this, and other matters, is embodied in the following report of a joint conference, the approval of which we recommend.

Atlanta, Nov. 2nd, 1899.

There was a joint conference of representatives of the different co-operative bodies engaged in work among the negroes in Georgia, held at the rooms of the Home Mission Board at 11 A. M. this day.

There were present, Brother McVicar, representing the A.B.H.M.S. of N.Y., Brethren Bell, Kerfoot, and Welch representing the Home Mission Board of Southern Baptist Convention, Brother Jameson, representing the Georgia State Board of Missions, and Brethren Carter, Bryan, and Johnson representing the Negro Educational Society of Georgia.

Brother Jameson was elected Chairman of the meeting and Brother Welch requested to act as Secretary.

Brother McVicar, by request, explained that the object of the meeting was to consider some slight changes in the Articles of Co-operation which were adopted Oct. 19th, 1898.

After full and free discussion certain amendments were agreed to, so that the amended copy of Articles of Co-operation which was unanimously adopted by the joint conference was as follows:

---

*Appendix II is reproduced with the written permission of the Home Mission Board of the Southern Baptist Convention, Atlanta, Georgia.

Articles Of Co-operation

These Articles were adopted October 18th, 1898, and were amended November 2nd, 1899. The bodies entering into co-operation and upon which they are binding, are The American Baptist Home Mission Society, the Home Board of the Southern Baptist Convention, the White Baptist State Convention of Georgia, and the Georgia Negro Baptist Education Society.

I. Object of Co-operation.

The object of this co-operation is to effect the strongest possible combination of talents and resources for the better organization and more efficient prosecution of Educational Missionary work among the Negro Baptists of the State of Georgia, and to make special provision for the education and training of the Negro ministry in the State, and for the Christian development of all the Baptist forces of the State.

II. Relations of Co-operative Bodies.

1. The co-operating bodies shall be co-ordinate, and shall have equal power and authority in all matters relating to the general policy and character of the work to be undertaken and the methods of its prosecution. These matters shall be decided by joint consultation of representatives of the co-operating bodies. The selection and appointment of all persons employed in carrying on the work of co-operation shall also be made by joint consultation of representatives of the co-operating bodies, and no formal overture shall be made to any person to fill a position until a joint decision has been reached.

2. Each co-operating body may issue its own commissions, and may pay its own proportion of salaries directly to the persons appointed.

3. At the end of each year each co-operating body shall report to the others the amounts it has paid to persons under joint appointment, and for incidental expenses of the plan of co-operation, with dates of payments.

4. In all meetings of the Education Society and of its Board of Managers, representatives of the other co-operating bodies shall have the privilege of participating in the deliberations.

5. The expenses of co-operation shall be borne as follows: For the first year one-fourth by each organization; for the second year one-third by the Education Society and two-thirds equally by the other organizations; and for the third year and after one-half by the Education Society, and the other half equally by the other organizations.

III. Nature of Work Undertaken.

1. To provide a practical system for the education and training of the large body of colored ministers in the State who have not been able to pursue any regular course of literary or theological studies.

2. To develop in the churches an intelligent and helpful interest in Christian education and missionary work, and to organize in them an effective plan of contributing systematically and liberally for these objects.

3. To look up young men and young women possessed of gifts and talents that will, if trained, make them useful to their race, and encourage such to attend the denominational schools in the State and also to get the churches, where necessary, to help them in doing so.

IV. Method of Doing the Work.

1. The State shall be divided into four districts, one of which shall be smaller than the other three, and shall be placed in charge of a General Educational Missionary, who shall supervise the entire work. The other three shall be placed in charge of three District Educational Missionaries.

2. The provision for the education and training of the ministry of the State shall be substantially as follows:

(a). A thorough English Theological Course shall be provided in Atlanta Baptist College, extending over six months each year, and requiring three years for its completion. The instruction in this course will require, for the six months, the services of two teachers, one of whom shall be provided and salary paid by the co-operating bodies, the other by the American Baptist Home Mission Society. The two Theological teachers in the college shall each devote four months each year to Institute work, under the direction of the General Educational Missionary.

(b). At central points, in each of the four districts into which the State shall be divided, at least six New Era Institutes, or Bible Schools, shall be conducted each year; each Institute continuing from three to ten days; during these days systematic and practical instruction shall be given on the following subjects: The Best Method of Studying the English Bible, and the Proper Use of Bible Helps; Biblical Theology; Church History; the Office and Work of the Christian Ministry; Home and Foreign Missions; Church Work, and Christian Education. The instruction in these subjects shall form a consecutive course of study extending over three years, and, when completed, shall entitle ministers and others who do the work to a certificate to that effect. The work in these Institutes, or Bible Schools, shall be performed by the Educational Missionaries, the teachers in theology in the college, and white and colored pastors in the neighborhood of the institutes, whose services can be secured to deliver one or more lectures at each Institute.

3. The other work of the co-operating bodies indicated under "Nature of Work Undertaken," in paragraphs 2 and 3, shall be performed by the Educational Missionaries, and the manner of doing the work shall be indicated in the statement of their duties.

Duties of Educational Missionaries.

1. The duties of the General Educational Missionary, who shall reside in the city of Atlanta, shall be substantially as follows:

(a). He shall have personal charge of the smallest of the four districts into which the State shall be divided, and in addition to the work of his own district he shall have the supervision and general charge of the entire work of the three District Missionaries.

(b). He shall, in conformity with the general policy adopted by the co-operating bodies, and under the direction of the Georgia Negro Baptist Education Society, and representatives of the other co-operating bodies, and in conference with the District Educational Missionaries, mature plans for effectively doing every part of the work undertaken by the co-operating bodies in every district of the State. He shall also supervise the execution of these plans by the District Missionaries, and be present and lecture at as many as possible of the Institutes or Bible Schools.

(c). He shall present the work of the co-operating bodies at the various Baptist State Conventions of Georgia; and also at as many associations as possible. He shall prepare and disseminate leaflets giving full information regarding the entire work; he shall, also, in co-operation with pastors and the District Missionaries, disseminate information regarding the work by holding mass meetings at central points throughout the State.

(d). He shall, in conference with the District missionaries, arrange the time and place for holding New Era Institutes or Bible Schools, and shall be present at as many of them as possible.

(e). He shall devise, in conference with the Board of Managers of the Education Society, and representatives of the other co-operating bodies, and the District Missionaries, a plan for raising money by the negro churches for that portion of the salaries of the Missionaries for which the Education Society is responsible, and for the support of teachers in the denominational schools adopted by the Education Society.

(f). He shall report monthly on his work to the Board of Managers of the Education Society, and make a formal quarterly report on blanks provided for that purpose to each of the co-operating bodies. He shall, however, make at any time such report or statement as may be required by any of the co-operating bodies.

2. The District Educational Missionaries shall each reside at a convenient point in the District of which he has charge, and they shall devote

their entire time and energy to their work, and their duties shall be substantially as follows:

(a). They shall execute every line of work undertaken by the co-operating bodies in conformity with the plans arranged by the General Educational Missionary, in conference with them and the Board of Managers of the Education Society and representatives of the other co-operating bodies.

(b). They shall give instructions in the New Era Institute, or Bible School, and for this work they must make careful, special preparation.

(c). They shall make special efforts to disseminate information in the churches regarding the work of the schools of the denomination in the State, and to induce Baptist young men and young women to attend these schools; and they shall also make special efforts to enlist the pastors in this work, and to induce the churches to contribute systematically and liberally for the support of teachers in the denominational schools. For this purpose they shall make themselves familiar with the work done in each of the denominational schools and shall visit churches and associations in their several districts, and hold mass meetings in connection with these churches and associations.

(d). They shall collect and report to the General Educational Missionary accurate information upon the following, namely: The amount of money contributed annually by churches, individuals and associations for educational and missionary work in the State; the number of associations in the State; the number of churches in each association; the number of members in each church, and the time and place of the meetings of the association.

(e). They shall report monthly, through the General Educational Missionary, the work done to the Board of Managers of the Education Society on blanks provided far [*sic*] that purpose.

VI. Care of Money Collected.

Each of the four Educational Missionaries shall deposit with the Treasurer of the Education Society, at the close of each month or quarter as may be agreed upon by the co-operating bodies, the entire amount of money collected during that time. Each must also take quadruplicate receipts from the Treasurer for the amount deposited, one of which must accompany his report to the Executive Committee of the Education Society and one must be attached to each of the reports to the other co-operating bodies.

VII. Cost of Co-operation.

The General Educational Missionary shall be paid for a year's service $800, and not to exceed $250 for expenses. Each of the three District Educational Missionaries shall be paid for a year's service $600, and not to exceed $150 for expenses. There shall be $300 allowed for Institute expenses. The Instructor in the Theological Department of Atlanta Baptist College shall be paid for his services not to exceed $1,000. His expenses when doing Institute or other work outside of the College shall be paid out of the $300 provided for Institute expenses. The aggregate salaries and expenses shall not exceed $4,600, and shall be paid as provided for under "Relation of Co-operating Bodies," as follows: The first year each of the Co-operating Bodies shall pay $1,150; the second year the Negro Baptist Education Society shall pay $1,533.33, and each of the other three bodies $1,022.22; and the third year and after the Education Society shall pay $2,300, and each of the other three bodies $766.66.

VIII. Amendments.

These Articles of Co-operation may be amended or changed as experience may suggest, but no change shall be made unless what is proposed is submitted in writing to the General Educational Missionary of the Co-operating bodies and to the Corresponding Secretary of each of the White Co-operating bodies. Upon motion of Brother Bell the following course of study and rules for conducting the Institutes was adopted.

Minister's New Era Institutes.
. . or . .
Bible Schools.

These Institutes, or Bible Schools, in the State of Georgia, are conducted under the auspices of the American Baptist Home Mission Society, the Home Board of the Southern Baptist Convention, the White Baptist State Convention, and the Georgia Negro Baptist Education Society, by four Educational Missionaries and a Theological Professor in the Atlanta Baptist College appointed and supported by these Co-operating Bodies.

Course of Instruction.

The aim of the instruction given in each Institute will be to render needed and efficient help to pastors by discussing with them practical methods of studying the English Bible, the preparation and delivery of sermons, and the best methods of organizing and successfully conducting every department of church work. The following will be the usual order of daily exercises pursued in each Institute:

1. The forenoon of each day will be given to special Bible study, accompanied by a half-hour lecture, and discussion by members of the Institute on selected topics; such as the following:

(a) Evidences of conversion as presented in the Scriptures, including the changed disposition and tastes, and growth in grace and knowledge.

(b) Christian stewardship in the use of money, and the sin of the misuse of funds given to the Lord.

(c) Loving obedience to Christ, or how love and law are related to each other in the Gospel.

(d) The value of good books to a minister; to give information; to stimulate thought; to cultivate the correct use of language; to give breadth of view, etc.

2. The afternoon of each day will be given to special preparation for the pulpit. This will include the selection and analysis of texts, the preparation and delivery of sermons, and the reading of Scripture and hymns. Members of the Institute will submit in writing, outlines of sermons, which will be read and discussed. This work will also be accompanied by a half-hour lecture, and discussion by members of the Institute on selected topics, such as the following:

(a) The qualifications, duties and obligations of ministers as presented in the First Epistle of Paul to Timothy.

(b) The Scriptural view of a Christian home, its power and influence in forming character.

(c) The organization and conduct of every department of church work, business meetings, prayer meetings, pastoral visitations, and Sunday School work.

3. A night session will be held at the close of each day, at which two half-hour lectures will usually be delivered on selected topics, such as the following. This will be followed by discussion by members of the Institute.

(a) Mission work in Cuba and Puerto Rico; its needs and present opportunities.

(b) The Home Mission Work of the Co-operating Bodies in Georgia and elsewhere.

(c) The kind and degree of education needed now, and for the coming generation, by the Colored people.

(d) The Baptist Schools for the Colored Baptists of Georgia; their origin, aims, and work.

The time that can be given to each Institute will vary from three days to two, or more weeks. It is hoped, however, that at many central points in the State, pastors and churches will co-operate in making it possible to continue each Institute for at least one or two weeks, which will prove more profitable than a shorter time.

Theological Reading Course.

The work of the Institutes, or Bible Schools, will be supplemented by the following three years course of Theological Reading. In connection with each Institute, or at some other convenient time, an oral or written examination will be given to such pastors and others as have completed one, or more, of the subjects of the course, and a card certifying to having passed the required test will be given by the Institute Conductors. When a card of this kind is secured for every subject of the course, a certificate will be given, signed by the Corresponding Secretaries of the four Co-operating Bodies.

The Theological Reading Course prescribed is as follows, subject, however, to such changes in matter as may be found desirable.

Course for the First Year.

1. *Bible Reading:*—The Gospel of Luke, the Acts of the Apostles, and the First Epistle of Paul to Timothy. These books are to be read and studied in connection with the analysis given of each, in "Bible Study by Books" by Rev. Henry T. Sell.

2. *Preparation of Sermons:*—The first twelve chapters of "The Making of the Sermon" by Rev. Prof. T. Harwood Pattison of the Rochester Theological Seminary.

3. *Baptist History:*—"A Short History of the Baptists" by Rev. Henry C. Vedder, Professor of Church History, in Crozer Theological Seminary.

4. *Supplementary Reading:*—The "Supplemental Bible Studies" by Rev. Henry T. Sell, the first fourteen chapters.

Course for the Second Year.

1. *Bible Reading:*—First and Second Samuel; the Gospel of St. Matthew; the Epistles of Paul to the Galatians and to the Ephesians. These two Epistles are to be studied doctrinally.

2. *Preparation of Sermons:*—The last eleven chapters of "The Making of the Sermon" by Rev. T. Harwood Pattison.

3. *Doctrinal Reading:*—"Bible Study by Doctrines" by Rev. Henry T. Sell. In reading this book the Bible references given are to be carefully considered and the outline of topics in each chapter fixed in the memory.

4. *Supplementary Reading:*—The "Supplemental Bible Study" by Rev. Henry T. Sell, the last ten chapters.

Course for the Third Year.

1. *Bible Study:*—The Book of Proverbs; and Prophecy of Isaiah; the Prophecy of Zechariah; the Epistle to the Hebrews; and the Book of Leviticus.

2. *Theological Reading:*—"Christian Doctrines" by Rev. J. M. Pendleton, D.D.

3. *Pastoral Theology:*—"The Pastor" by H. Harvey, D.D.; "How to be a Pastor" by Theodore L. Cuyler, D.D.

4. *Church Organization:*—"The Church" by Rev. H. Harvey, D.D.

NOTES

Abbreviations

ESB	*Encyclopedia of Southern Baptists*
Minutes HMB	Minutes of the Home Mission Board
HF	*Our Home Field* and *The Home Field*
SBC	Southern Baptist Convention
SBHLA	Southern Baptist Historical Library and Archives
Tichenor Diary	Isaac Taylor Tichenor Diary

1. Reclaiming a Legacy: An Assessment of Southern Baptists and the Social Gospel

1. C. Vann Woodward, *Origins of the New South, 1877–1913* (Baton Rouge: Louisiana State University Press, 1951), 450.

2. C. Howard Hopkins, *The Rise of the Social Gospel in American Protestantism, 1865–1915* (New Haven: Yale University Press, 1940). For an updated revision of this work see Ronald C. White, Jr., and C. Howard Hopkins, *The Social Gospel—Religion and Reform in a Changing America* (Philadelphia: Temple University Press, 1976), especially 80–96, which look at the rural South.

3. Henry F. May, *Protestant Churches in Industrial America* (New York: Harper and Brothers, 1949), passim, especially 163–263.

4. Robert T. Handy, ed., *The Social Gospel in America* (New York: Oxford University Press, 1966), 4. See also Timothy L. Smith, *Revivalism and Social Reform: American Protestantism on the Eve of the Civil War* (Nashville: Abingdon Press, 1957).

5. See as examples Samuel S. Hill, Jr., ed., *Religion in the Solid South* (Nashville: Abingdon Press, 1972); and Charles Reagan Wilson, ed., *Religion in the South*, The Chancellor's Symposium series, (Jackson: University Press of Mississippi, 1985).

6. Kenneth K. Bailey, *Southern White Protestantism in the Twentieth-Century South* (New York: Harper & Row, 1964), 42.

7. Rufus B. Spain, *At Ease in Zion: A Social History of Southern Baptists, 1865–1900* (Nashville: Vanderbilt University Press, 1967), 210–11.

8. Ibid., 212.

9. John Lee Eighmy, *Churches in Cultural Captivity: A History of the Social Attitudes of Southern Baptists*, with revised introduction, conclusion, and bibliography, 1987, by Samuel S. Hill (1972; reprint, Knoxville: University of Tennessee Press, 1987).

10. Samuel S. Hill, Jr., *The South and the North in American Religion*, Lamar Memorial Lectures, Mercer University, no. 23 (Athens: University of Georgia Press, 1980).

11. Samuel S. Hill, Jr., *Southern Churches in Crisis* (New York: Holt, Rinehart & Winston, 1966), 171.

12. James J. Thompson, Jr., *Tried as by Fire: Southern Baptists and the Religious Controversies of the 1920s* (Macon: Mercer University Press, 1982).

13. John B. Boles, "The Discovery of a Southern Religious History," in *Interpreting Southern History*, ed. John B. Boles and Evelyn Thomas Nolen (Baton Rouge: Louisiana State University Press, 1987), 540–41.

14. For an impressive work dealing with Baptist women see Catherine B. Allen, *A Century to Celebrate: History of Women's Missionary Union* (Birmingham: Women's Missionary Union, 1987). For other interesting works not directly dealing with Baptists see Anne F. Scott, "Women, Religion, and Social Change in the South, 1830–1930," in *Religion in the Solid South*, ed. Samuel S. Hill, Jr., 92–121; Ruth Brigitta Anderson Bordin, *Women and Temperance: The Quest for Power and Liberty, 1873–1900* (Philadelphia: Temple University Press, 1981); Ruth Brigitta Anderson Bordin, *Frances Willard: A Biography* (Chapel Hill: University of North Carolina Press, 1986); Jacquelyn Dowd Hall, *Revolt Against Chivalry: Jessie Daniel Ames and the Women's Campaign Against Lynching* (New York: Columbia University Press, 1979); John Patrick McDowell, *The Social Gospel in the South: The Women's Home Mission Movement in the Methodist Episcopal Church, South, 1886–1939* (Baton Rouge: Louisiana State University Press, 1982).

15. Wayne Flynt, "Dissent in Zion: Alabama Baptists and Social Issues, 1900–1914," *Journal of Southern History* 35 (winter 1969): 523–42.

16. J. Wayne Flynt, " 'Feeding the Hungry and Ministering to the Broken Hearted': The Presbyterian Church in the United States and the Social Gospel, 1900–1920," in *Religion in the South*, ed. Charles Reagan Wilson, The Chancellor's Symposium series (Jackson: University Press of Mississippi, 1985), 83–137.

17. John W. Storey, *Texas Baptist Leadership and Social Christianity, 1900–1980* (College Station: Texas A&M Press, 1986).

18. Wayne Flynt, "Southern Baptists and Reform: 1890–1920," *Baptist History and Heritage* 7 (October 1972): 212–13.

19. May, *Protestant Churches in Industrial America*, 170. See the footnote.

20. Sidney E. Mead, *The Lively Experiment: The Shaping of Christianity in America* (New York: Harper & Row, 1976), 178.

21. Handy, *The Social Gospel in America*, 5–6.

22. See Liston Pope, *Millhands and Preachers* (New Haven: Yale University Press, 1942). This work is informative and interesting, but dated. For a description of socioeconomic change introduced by industrialization see Wayne Flynt, *Poor but Proud* (Tuscaloosa: University of Alabama Press, 1989), and Ronald D Eller, *Miners, Millhands, and Mountaineers: Industrialization of the Appalachian South, 1880–1930* (Knoxville: University of Tennessee Press, 1982).

23. Mead, *The Lively Experiment*, 177–78.

24. Robert D. Linder, "The Resurgency of Evangelical Social Concern (1925–1975)," in *The Evangelicals*, ed. David F. Wells and John D. Woodbridge (Nashville: Abingdon Press, 1975; reprint, Grand Rapids: Baker Book House, 1977), 226–27 n. 6.

25. Ibid., 227. Samuel S. Hill noted this distinction in the 1987 edition of John Eighmy's *Churches in Cultural Captivity*. Hill wrote the introduction, conclusion, and bibliography to this work because Eighmy had suffered a fatal heart attack in 1970. At any rate, Hill said that Southern Baptists manifested considerable social

concern and social ministry, but little social action (see Hill's introduction to *Churches in Cultural Captivity*, xii–xiii).

26. Eighmy, *Churches in Cultural Captivity*, xx.

27. Joel Williamson, *The Crucible of Race* (New York: Oxford University Press, 1984), 24–35.

28. Ibid., 24.

29. Ibid. Williamson's work focused on race relations, but the concept of place-ness is equally true of whites. *Everyone* needed to find their place.

30. Donald G. Matthews, "The Second Great Awakening as an Organizing Process, 1780–1830: An Hypothesis," *American Quarterly* 21 (spring 1969): 31.

31. Robert A. Baker, *The Southern Baptist Convention and Its People, 1607–1972* (Nashville: Broadman Press, 1974), 204–7.

32. Lynn E. May, Jr., "Southern Baptist Social Consciousness, 1845–1855" (master's thesis, Vanderbilt University, 1968).

2. Reaching the Dispossessed: Southern Baptist Missions and Movement Culture

1. Baker, *Southern Baptist Convention*, 257.

2. Ibid., 287–319. See also H. Leon McBeth, *The Baptist Heritage: Four Centuries of Baptist Witness* (Nashville: Broadman Press, 1987), 392–463.

3. McBeth, *The Baptist Heritage*, 463.

4. Lawrence Goodwyn, *Democratic Promise: The Populist Movement in America* (New York: Oxford University Press, 1976), 3–109. See also Goodwyn's, *The Populist Moment* (New York: Oxford University Press, 1978), 3–54. For more information on Populism's antecedents see Robert C. McMath, Jr., *Populist Vanguard: A History of the Southern Farmers' Alliance* (New York: W. W. Norton, 1977). For an analysis of southern poverty see Wayne Flynt, *Poor but Proud: Alabama's Poor Whites* (Tuscaloosa: University of Alabama Press, 1989).

5. Goodwyn, *The Populist Moment*, 35.

6. Ibid., 20–54.

7. Ibid. For the religious aspects of Populism's antecedents see McMath, *Populist Vanguard*, 75–76.

8. McMath, *Populist Vanguard*, 76.

9. Goodwyn, *The Populist Moment*, 20–54.

10. Ibid., xix.

11. Frank S. Mead, *Handbook of Denominations in the United States*, 6th ed. (Nashville: Abingdon Press, 1975), 38.

12. *Encyclopedia of Southern Baptists*, s.v. "Church," by Theron D. Price (Nashville: Broadman Press, 1958) hereafter cited as *ESB*.

13. *ESB*, s.v. "Association, The District," by E. C. Routh.

14. *ESB*, s.v. "Convention, The State," by E. C. Routh.

15. Ibid.

16. *ESB*, s.v. "Southern Baptist Convention," by J. W. Storer.

17. Bill J. Leonard, *God's Last and Only Hope* (Grand Rapids: William B. Eerdmans Publishing, 1990), 113–22. For an excellent example of another religious group which thrived within the South's late nineteenth-century movement culture

see Mickey Crews, *The Church of God—A Social History* (Knoxville: University of Tennessee Press, 1990).

18. E. Y. Mullins, "The Crisis in Home Missions," *Our Home Field* XVIII (January 1907): 13. Between 1888 and 1909, *The Home Field* was published under the title *Our Home Field*. The name was changed in 1909, and it remained the official "voice" of the Home Mission Board until 1916. Hereafter, this publication will be cited as *HF*.

19. B. D. Gray and J. F. Love, eds., "Editorial," *HF* XVIII (October 1906): 3.

20. Ibid. Notice particularly p. 6 and the information under the heading, "The South and the Baptists."

21. William Louis Poteat, "Christianity and Society," *The Biblical Recorder*, August 16, 1905, 1.

22. Ibid.

23. Ibid.

24. "Editorial," *HF* XXV (January 1914): 23.

25. Ibid.

26. William J. McGlothlin, "The Seminary and Mountain and Frontier Missions," *HF* XXI (October 1909): 3–4.

27. Charles Spurgeon Gardner, "Home Missions and Social Improvement," *HF* XXI (November 1909): 4.

28. Ibid.

29. A. E. Brown, "Our Mountain Schools—Are They Worthwhile?" *HF* XXII (April 1911): 5.

30. Ibid.

31. J. S. Dill, "Missions in the Southern States," pamphlet published by The Maryland Baptist Mission Rooms, October 1894, 2–3.

32. Ibid., 3.

33. Ibid., 4. There is no doubt that "our religion" was southern white Protestantism in the form of Southern Baptist dogma.

34. "Editorial," *HF* XVIII (January 1907): 3.

35. Ibid.

36. A. E. Brown, "Our Mountain Schools—Are They Worthwhile?" 5.

37. R. R. Acree, "Testimonial," Una Roberts Lawrence Collection, Southern Baptist Historical Library and Archives (SBHLA), Nashville, Tennessee, Box 16, Folder 29.

38. One of the leading biblical qualifications for the office of deacon is hospitality; see 1 Timothy 3:2.

39. Gardner, "Home Missions and Social Improvement," 3.

40. Ibid., 4.

41. James W. Durham, "The Christianization of the South," *HF* XXIII (February 1912): 19.

42. Ibid., 20.

43. See as examples Arthur S. Link, "The Progressive Movement in the South, 1870-1914," *North Carolina Historical Review* 23 (April 1946): 172–95; Hugh C. Bailey, *Edgar Gardner Murphy—Gentle Progressive* (Coral Gables: University of Miami Press, 1968); and Hugh C. Bailey, *Liberalism in the New South: Southern Social Reformers and the Progressive Movement* (Coral Gables: University of Miami Press, 1969).

3. Preachers and Prelates: Southern Baptist
Leadership and the Emergence of a Social Ethic

1. *Annual*, Southern Baptist Convention, 1913, 60.

2. Ibid., 61. The implication here is that the first-rate institution was to be Baptist.

3. Kenneth K. Bailey, *Southern White Protestantism in the Twentieth-Century South*, 26.

4. *ESB*, s.v. "Southern Baptist Theological Seminary," by Leo T. Crismon. See also *ESB*, s.v. "Boyce, James Petigru," by Hugh Wamble.

5. Archibald Thomas Robertson, ed., *Life and Letters of John Albert Broadus* (Philadelphia: American Baptist Publication Society, 1901), 352–54.

6. *ESB*, s.v. "Gardner, Charles Spurgeon," by Leo T. Crismon.

7. *Annual*, Kentucky, 1912, 11–14.

8. Ibid.

9. Charles Spurgeon Gardner, *The Ethics of Jesus and Social Progress* (New York: George H. Doran, 1914), 19.

10. Ibid., 65–82.

11. Ibid., 107–9.

12. Ibid., 139–43.

13. Ibid., 211–16.

14. Ibid., 284.

15. Ibid., 297–304.

16. Ibid., 356.

17. *ESB*, s.v. "Eager, George Broadman," by Gaines S. Dobbins.

18. George Broadman Eager, *Lectures in Ecclesiology* (Louisville: Mayes Printing, 1917, printed for students), 25.

19. Ibid.

20. Ibid., 26.

21. Ibid., 27.

22. Robert A. Baker, *Tell the Generations Following: A History of Southwestern Baptist Theological Seminary, 1908–1983* (Nashville: Broadman Press, 1983), passim. See also McBeth, *The Baptist Heritage*, 668–69.

23. *ESB*, s.v. "Carroll, Benajah Harvey," by Franklin M. Segler. See also B. H. Carroll, *An Interpretation of the English Bible* (hereafter cited as *Interpretation*). This set was originally published by Fleming H. Revell Company in 1913. Broadman Press purchased the copyright in 1942 and added four volumes to complete the set. In 1973, Baker Book House reprinted the complete *Interpretation* in six volumes. They reissued the six-volume set again in 1976. This study uses the 1976 edition.

24. McBeth, *The Baptist Heritage*, 670.

25. Carroll, *Interpretation*, "The Hebrew Monarchy," 62.

26. Carroll, *Interpretation*, "James, Thessalonians, Corinthians," 27.

27. *Buckner Bulletin*, October 1954, vol. 2, no. 4, 1.

28. Carroll, *Interpretation*, "The Gospels," pt. 1, 365.

29. Ibid., 371.

30. *ESB*, s.v. "Tichenor, Isaac Taylor," by Kimball Johnson.

31. Ibid. See also Baker, *Southern Baptist Convention*, 261–64.

32. Isaac Taylor Tichenor Diary, see sermon, "Claims of the Bible Upon the Consideration of All Men," 1–2. Isaac Taylor Tichenor Papers, Southern Baptist Theological Seminary, Louisville, Kentucky. This material includes a portion of Tichenor's diary from 1850, his reminiscences of Shiloh, his reports to the Board of Directors while he was president of Alabama's Agriculture and Mechanical College, and a memorial by Lansing Burrows. Hereafter cited as Tichenor Diary.

33. Ibid., p. 4 of sermon.

34. Ibid., p. 12 of sermon.

35. Tichenor Diary, November 11, 1850.

36. Tichenor Diary, November 27, 1850.

37. Tichenor Diary, December 1, 6, 1850.

38. Tichenor Diary, December 14, 1850.

39. Tichenor Diary, "A Message on Hebrews 12:1–2," passim.

40. Tichenor Diary, "Religious Progress," passim, especially 19.

41. Tichenor Diary, "Second Report Submitted at the Annual Meeting of the Board of Directors," July 30, 1873, 7–8.

42. Tichenor Diary, "The Fifth Report," January 8, 1877, 32. (Tichenor's emphasis).

43. Ibid., 36–37.

44. Tichenor Diary, "The Sixth Report," June 24, 1878, 72.

45. Tichenor Diary, "Report to the Governor of the State," October 10, 1876, passim, especially 46.

46. Tichenor Diary, "Tenth Report," June 27, 1881, 115.

47. Tichenor Diary, "Sixth Report," June 25, 1877, 60. Tichenor's daughter, Kate Tichenor Dill, was interviewed in 1944, when she was nearly 88 years old. She said her father owned about a half-dozen slaves; see Diary, "Reminisces of Shiloh."

48. Tichenor Diary, "Sixth Report," June 25, 1877, 62. For a fuller account of the Southern Baptist Sunday School Board, see H. Leon McBeth, *The Baptist Heritage*, 432–40.

49. Lansing Burrows, *Tichenor Memorial of the Church Building Loan Fund* (Baltimore: Women's Missionary Union, 1903), 5 (Burrows's emphasis).

50. *Annual*, SBC, 1885, xv–xvi.

51. Burrows, *Tichenor Memorial of the Church Building Loan Fund*, 5.

52. Baker, *Southern Baptist Convention*, 263.

53. Paul M. Gaston, *The New South Creed: A Study in Southern Mythmaking* (New York: Alfred A. Knopf, 1970), 50.

54. Richard H. Edmunds, "Baptist Opportunity in the Growing South," *HF* XXI (June 1910): 3.

55. Ibid., 4.

56. Ibid., 6.

57. See 1 Corinthians 4:1–6.

58. "Editorial," *HF* XVIII (March 1907): 4.

59. See *The Western Recorder*, January 3, 1889, 1. The *Recorder* noted, "God's method of saving this world is by a saved church. Pentecostal baptisms bring Pentecostal reformations." This quote was copied.

60. Victor I. Masters, "The Church and Social Unrest," *HF* XXIII (January 1912): 10.

61. Ibid., 12.

62. Ibid., 14.

63. Richard H. Edmunds, "The Pulpit and Sociology," *HF* XXIII (February 1912): 25–26.

4. Southern Baptists, Social Christianity, and Orphanages

1. *Annual,* Mississippi, 1870, 34–35. See also *ESB,* s.v. "Mississippi Baptist Orphanage," by W. C. Cathey.
2. *Annual,* Mississippi, 1867, 29–31. See also *Annual,* Mississippi, 1868, 34.
3. Ibid., 36.
4. Ibid.
5. Ibid., 35.
6. Grace Lewis Hardaway, *A History of the Louisville Baptist Orphans Home* (n.p., n.d.), 3. The facility will hereafter be referred to as L.B.O.H. This work is a short narrative of the Home's early history and was prepared for its sixtieth anniversary in 1929. It is on file at Spring Meadows Children's Home, Louisville, Kentucky.
7. Ibid.
8. Ibid. See also *Brief History of Spring Meadows* (n.p., n.d.), on file at Spring Meadows Children's Home, Louisville, Kentucky.
9. Bernard Washington Spilman, *The Mills Home* (Thomasville, N.C.: Mills Home, 1932), 1–26.
10. *The Biblical Recorder,* July 16, 1884, 2.
11. *The Biblical Recorder,* July 30, 1884, 2.
12. Spilman, *The Mills Home,* 39–40. See also Alan Keith-Lucas, *A Hundred Years of Caring* (Thomasville, N.C.: Baptist Children's Homes of North Carolina, 1985), 1–2.
13. Spilman, *The Mills Home,* 46–47; and Keith-Lucas, *A Hundred Years of Caring,* 2.
14. Spilman, *The Mills Home,* 39.
15. J. B. Cranfill and J. L. Walker, *R. C. Buckner's Life of Faith and Works* (1914; reprinted and enlarged, Dallas: Buckner Orphans' Home, 1916), passim.
16. See the *ESB* for information on respective states. See also the state *Annuals* for specific years. Mississippi and Georgia are examples of states who reopened orphanages.
17. Baker, *Southern Baptist Convention,* 287–319. See also McBeth, *The Baptist Heritage,* 392–463; and W. W. Barnes, *The Southern Baptist Convention* (Nashville: Broadman Press, 1954), 166–79.
18. *Annual,* Georgia, 1900, 64.
19. A. T. Jamison, *Forty Years of Connie Maxwell History* (Greenwood: Board of Trustees, Connie Maxwell Orphanage, 1932), 8–9. See also the *Annual,* South Carolina, 1892.
20. *Annual,* Alabama, 1899, 22.
21. Buckner to Dinwiddie, R. C. Buckner's Papers, File no. 84–007 at Southwestern Baptist Theological Seminary, Fort Worth, Texas.
22. *Annual,* Tennessee, 1896, 25.
23. Alan Keith-Lucas, *A History of Connie Maxwell Children's Home, 1892–1977* (Greenwood: Connie Maxwell Children's Home, 1982), 3. See also Jamison, *Forty Years of Connie Maxwell History,* 1–9.

24. *The Buckner Orphans Home Annual,* 1905–1906, 27. The Buckner Home published these reports yearly.

25. See the Finance Committee Report, L.B.O.H., 1914, and Minutes of the Board of Male Managers, L.B.O.H., 1914, 162–65, on file at Spring Meadows Children's Home, Louisville, Kentucky. These sources indicate that the endowment had grown steadily from $192,700 in 1909, to $303,640 in 1914. Finances at the Louisville Baptist Orphans Home were atypical.

26. *Annual,* South Carolina, 1892–1920. The Connie Maxwell Children's Home reports are of particular importance here.

27. Thomas E. Pugh, *As a Grain of Mustard Seed* (Roanoke: Progress Press, 1983), 15–16. See also A. T. Jamison, *Forty Years of Connie Maxwell History,* 181–85.

28. Jamison, *Forty Years,* 185–86.

29. *Annual,* Maryland, 1920, 36–37. See also *History of the Baptist Home for Children* (n.p.), May 20, 1990.

30. *The Buckner Orphans Home Annual,* 1891–1892, 3–4.

31. Ibid.

32. See especially Mary A. Hollingsworth, "Adopting Children," *The Orphan's Friend* 1 (February 1872): 1. This early example is cited because it established a precedent. Other homes had similar stipulations.

33. Ibid.

34. *The Buckner Orphans Home Annual,* 1906–1907, 26.

35. *Annual,* Tennessee, 1911, 35.

36. Mary A. Hollingsworth, "Education," *The Orphan's Friend* 1 (March 1872): 1.

37. Mary A. Hollingsworth, "An Amusing Incident," *The Orphan's Friend* 1 (April 1872): 2. Quoted as recounted by the editors.

38. *Annual,* Kentucky, 1915, 54–60.

39. Spilman, *The Mills Home,* 50.

40. A. T. Jamison, *The Institution for Children* (Columbia: Baptist Book Depository, 1926), 57–58.

41. Jamison, *Forty Years,* 186; and *Annual,* Alabama, 1903, 21.

42. *Annual,* Tennessee, 1909, 18–20.

43. Ibid., 21.

44. Jamison, *The Institution for Children,* 47.

45. *Annual,* Georgia, 1902, 78.

46. Ibid., 1911, 111.

47. Ibid., 1914, 97, and 1920, 92.

48. Spilman, *The Mills Home,* 95. See also *Annual,* Mississippi, 1910, 29; and Jamison, *Forty Years,* 140–41.

49. Mary A. Hollingsworth, "Our Infirmary," *The Orphan's Friend* 2 (May 1873): 2.

50. *Annual,* Kentucky, 1910, 59–60.

51. *Annual,* Mississippi, 1914, 42.

52. David J. Rothman, *The Discovery of the Asylum* (Boston: Little, Brown, 1971), xxiii.

53. Ibid., passim, especially 71 and 217–20.

54. Priscilla Ferguson Clement, "Families and Foster Care: Philadelphia in the Late Nineteenth Century," in *Growing Up in America,* ed. N. Ray Hiner and Joseph M. Hawes (Urbana: University of Illinois Press, 1985), 135–46. For other discussions of this problem see Anthony M. Platt, *The Child Savers,* 2d ed. (Chi-

cago: University of Chicago Press, 1977). David J. Rothman also examines the transition from rehabilitation to custodialism in American asylums in *Conscience and Convenience* (Boston: Little, Brown, 1980).

55. Clement, "Families and Foster Care," 138.

56. David Brion Davis, *Antebellum American Culture* (Lexington, Mass.: D. C. Heath, 1979), 1–8.

57. Rothman, *The Discovery of the Asylum*, 212.

58. Jamison, *The Institution for Children*, 17.

59. Ibid., 58.

60. Ibid., 10–21.

61. Ibid., 53–54.

62. Jamison, *Forty Years*, 103.

63. Buckner, *The Buckner Orphans Home Annual* 1905–1906, 36. Whether this constitutes social control or stands as an example of genuine humanitarian concern is perhaps debatable. In the introduction to *The Bible and Social Reform*, Ernest R. Sandeen correctly observes that the "social control" thesis was generated in part by the cynical political climate of the 1960s and 1970s. He cites Paul Boyer's *Urban Masses and Moral Order in America, 1820–1920* as an example of a more dispassionate approach to reformers. Boyer contends that reformers usually strove to restore "social equilibrium" either by recapturing the past or through a plan of their own. For Baptists, this meant emphasizing the home/family as a socially stable unit. The significant thing is that Baptist orphanages tried to instill morality and virtue in orphans through an individual approach. The emphasized individual dignity and self-worth. Their insistence upon making each orphanage a home necessitated their viewing each child differently. It was not possible for them to develop a single plan by which they could deal with all children.

64. *Annual*, Alabama, 1899, 22.

65. Spilman, *The Mills Home*, 56. Mills was later instrumental in the establishing of a school for the feebleminded in the mid-1890s in Lenoir County.

66. Rothman, *The Discovery of the Asylum*, 217.

67. *Annual*, Mississippi, 1914, 68.

5. Redeeming the Mountaineers: Southern Baptists and Mountain Mission Schools

1. Dewey W. Grantham, "The Contours of Southern Progressivism," *American Historical Review* 86 (December 1981): 1047. See also Dewey W. Grantham, *Southern Progressivism: The Reconciliation of Tradition and Progress* (Knoxville: University of Tennessee Press, 1983), 246–74.

2. Grantham, "The Contours of Southern Progressivism," 1039.

3. Henry D. Shapiro, *Appalachia on Our Mind: The Southern Mountains and Mountaineers in the American Conscience, 1870–1920* (Chapel Hill: University of North Carolina Press, 1978), 32–58, especially 33. See also Joe M. Richardson, *Christian Reconstruction* (Athens: University of Georgia Press, 1986).

4. Shapiro, *Appalachia on Our Mind*, 57.

5. John E. White, "The Southern Mountaineer," *HF* XXI (August 1909): 16.

6. Ibid.

7. Ibid., 15.

8. Ibid., 17.

9. Stephen B. Weeks, *History of Public School Education in Alabama* (Washington, D.C.: Government Printing Office, 1915), bulletin no. 12, whole no. 637, 132–34. Even at this, the per capita apportionment amounted to less than one dollar per child.

10. H. C. Bailey, *Liberalism in the New South*, 33.

11. Ellis Ford Hartford, *The Little White Schoolhouse* (Lexington: University of Kentucky Press, 1977), 10.

12. Grantham, *Southern Progressivism*, 257.

13. Ibid., table no. 10, 258.

14. Ibid., 22.

15. Ibid., 84–85.

16. Charles William Dabney, *Universal Education in the South*, vol 2 (Chapel Hill: University of North Carolina Press, 1936), 219.

17. William Elijah Robinson, "The Elbridge (Alabama) Baptist Academy" (master's Ed. thesis, College of Education, University of Alabama, 1947), 11.

18. Dabney, *Universal Education*, 219.

19. Grantham, *Southern Progressivism*, 258.

20. *ESB*, s.v. "Mountain Mission Schools," by A. B. Cash.

21. Ibid.

22. Victor I. Masters, *The Home Mission Task* (Atlanta: Blosser, 1912), 224.

23. *Annual*, SBC, 1900, 41–42.

24. Ibid.

25. Ibid.

26. *ESB*, s.v. "Brown, Albert Erskine," by W. H. Williams.

27. Osie Allison, "Testimonial," Una Roberts Lawrence Collection, SBHLA, Nashville, Tennessee, Box 16, folder 1.

28. *Minutes of the Home Mission Board*, May 19, July 5, 1904 (hereafter cited as *Minutes HMB*). See also *ESB*, s.v. "Brown, Albert Erskine," by W. H. Williams.

29. *Minutes HMB*, January 2, 1906. See also *Minutes HMB*, June 11, 1907, under the heading, "An Appreciation," and the financial statement for 1912.

30. *Minutes HMB*, October 3, 1905.

31. *Minutes HMB*, July 5, 1905.

32. *Minutes HMB*, July 5, 1909.

33. See Appendix I. These numbers do not include those schools that received aid from the Home Mission Board on a temporary basis.

34. *Minutes HMB*, September 3, 1912.

35. *Minutes HMB*, September 10, 1903.

36. *Minutes HMB*, September 10, 1903, and December 12, 1899. For more information about Stockton's Valley Institute see Fred Sanders's account of Stockton's Valley, Una Roberts Lawrence Collection, SBHLA, Nashville, Tennessee, Box 16, folder 29. Even though some of these transactions predate A. E. Brown, policies did not differ significantly once he became superintendent of the Mountain Schools.

37. John E. White, "Ten Years of Partnership," *HF* XXI (October 1909): 11.

38. Ibid., 11–12.

39. John Angus McLeod, *From These Stones—Mars Hill College 1856–1967* (1955; revised ed., Mars Hill, N.C.: Mars Hill College, 1968), 204.

40. White, "Ten Years of Partnership," 12.

41. A. E. Brown, *Southern Baptist Mountain School Work* (Atlanta: Home Mission Board of the Southern Baptist Convention, 1908–09).

42. A. E. Brown, "Progress Among the Mountain Schools," *HF* XXIV (April 1913): 16.

43. See W. J. Berry, *ESB*, s.v. "Primitive Baptists."

44. A. E. Brown, "Tact and Love Win a Hardshell Church," *HF* XXVI (October 1915): 5.

45. *Annual*, SBC, 1900, 40–43.

46. *Annual Leaflet, Home Mission Board of the Southern Baptist Convention* (Baltimore: Baptist Mission Rooms, 1899), 5–6.

47. A. E. Brown, "Mountain School Notes," *HF* XXII (December 1910): 15.

48. A. E. Brown, "The Mission and Value of Our Mountain Schools," *Home and Foreign Fields* 3 (March 1919): 6–7.

49. Oscar M. Drennen, "Testimonial," Una Roberts Lawrence Collection, SBHLA, Nashville, Tennessee, Box 16, folder 37.

50. Allison, "Testimonial."

51. Ibid., 4.

52. Ibid., 5.

53. Ibid., 5 (no specific date mentioned).

54. Ibid., 9.

55. Ibid., 9–10.

56. Ibid., 9.

57. A. E. Brown, "Our Mountain Schools—Are They Worthwhile?" 5.

58. Ibid.

59. Ibid., 6.

60. A. E. Brown, "Notes from Superintendent Brown," *HF* XVIII (November 1906): 7.

61. A. E. Brown, "Mountain Schools," *HF* XVIII (May 1907): 12.

62. Grantham, "The Contours of Southern Progressivism," 1035–59.

63. Ibid., 1050.

64. Victor I. Masters, "The Mountain People," *HF* XX (April 1909): 19, (emphasis added).

65. Ibid.

66. George B. Tindall, "Business Progressivism: Southern Politics in the Twenties," *The South Atlantic Quarterly* 62 (1963): 93–106.

67. Ronald D Eller, *Miners, Millhands, and Mountaineers*, 110–12.

68. Woodward, *Origins of the New South*, 369–95.

6. Of Leopard Spots and Ethiopian Skin: Southern Baptists and Racial Uplift

1. Joel Williamson, *The Crucible of Race: Black-White Relations in the American South since Emancipation* (New York: Oxford University Press, 1984), 11–110.

2. Ibid., 4.

3. Ibid., 5–6.

4. Ibid., 6.

5. Ibid.

6. Eric Foner, *Reconstruction: America's Unfinished Revolution*, The New American Nation series (New York: Harper & Row, 1988), 89. See also Howard N. Rabinowitz, *Race Relations in the Urban South, 1865–1890*, Blacks in the New

World series (New York: Oxford University Press, 1978; reprint, Illini Books edition, Urbana: University of Illinois Press, 1980), 198–225.

7. Foner, *Reconstruction*, 92.

8. Ibid., 89–94. See also Rabinowitz, *Race Relations in the Urban South*, 198–225.

9. Edward L. Wheeler, *Uplifting the Race* (Lanham, Md.: University Press of America, 1986), xii–xiii. Wheeler's work focuses primarily on 78 southern black ministers whom he identifies as a self-conscious elite within the black community.

10. Ibid., xiii.

11. Ibid.

12. Ibid., 17.

13. "Report of Committee on Education of Proper Kind of Negro Preachers," *Minutes of the Spartanburg Baptist Association*, 1894, 5–6.

14. H. L. McBeth, *The Baptist Heritage*, 429. See also Robert A. Baker, *Relations Between Northern and Southern Baptists* (1954; reprint, New York: Arno Press, 1980), 144–70.

15. Baker, *Relations Between Northern and Southern Baptists*, 144–70.

16. *Minutes HMB*, December 21, 1888.

17. *Minutes HMB*, April, 1889.

18. McBeth, *The Baptist Heritage*, 430.

19. *Annual*, SBC, 1892, Appendix A, xi.

20. *Annual*, SBC, 1894, 16.

21. *Annual*, SBC, 1895, 14–16. See also McBeth, *The Baptist Heritage*, 430–31, and Baker, *Southern Baptist Convention*, 265–66.

22. McBeth, *The Baptist Heritage*, 431.

23. *Minutes HMB*, September 24, 1894. See also chap. 2 in this work.

24. *Minutes HMB*, February 1, 1898. One year later the Home Board refused this recommendation, arguing that without aid from the state's mission board, it was inadvisable to "undertake any part of the co-operative work among the Negroes in that state."

25. *Minutes HMB*, February 9, 1899.

26. *Minutes HMB*, November 2, 1899. The conditions of this joint agreement are reproduced in Appendix II of this work.

27. Ibid.

28. *Minutes HMB*, January 2, 1900. See also James M. McPherson, "White Liberals and Black Power in Negro Education, 1865–1915," *American Historical Review* 75 (June 1970): 1357–86.

29. Ibid.

30. *ESB*, s.v. "Negroes, Southern Baptist Relations to," by Courts Redford.

31. James O. Buswell III, *Slavery, Segregation and Scripture* (Grand Rapids: William B. Eerdmans, 1964), 19–25. See Genesis 9:18–27.

32. Ibid., 23–24.

33. D. L. Gore, "The Negro Race," *HF* XXII (July 1911): 5. Gore's family had owned slaves before the Civil War. In 1911, he employed some 200 black persons on his farm.

34. Ibid.

35. Ibid.

36. Ibid.

37. Ibid. This is an unusual criticism of what Williamson calls the "New Ne-

gro." The Baptist press usually had little to say about "town dudes." Rather, they extolled the virtues of those blacks they deemed praiseworthy and ignored all others. Criticism, when offered, was usually restrained.

38. C. C. Brown, "A Suggested Solution to a Sore Problem," *HF* XXII (September 1910): 9. See also *ESB*, s.v. "Brown, Clinton Capers," by William R. McLin.

39. Ibid.

40. Ibid.

41. J. B. Gambrell, "The South's Obligation to the Negroes," *HF* XXII (September 1910): 5.

42. Ibid., 3.

43. "Editorial," *HF* XXII (September 1910): 19.

44. Gambrell, "The South's Obligation to the Negroes," 4.

45. Wayne Flynt, "The Negro and Alabama Baptists During the Progressive Era," *Journal of the Alabama Academy of Science* 39 (April 1968): 165. See also Gambrell, "The South's Obligation to the Negroes," 3–4.

46. B. F. Riley, "Our Obligation to the Negro," *HF* XXII (September 1910): 10–11. See also *ESB*, s.v. "Riley, Benjamin Franklin," by Terry L. Jones, supplement vol. 3.

47. C. C. Brown, "A Suggested Solution for a Sore Problem," 9.

48. Ibid., 9–10.

49. Ibid., 11.

50. Weston Bruner, "Southern Baptists and Negro Baptists," *HF* XXIV (December 1913): 13. See also *ESB*, s.v. "Bruner, Weston" by John F. Havlik, supplement vol. 3.

51. Ibid.

52. E. C. Morris, "Dr. C. C. Brown and the Negro," *HF* XXVII (June 1916): 12.

53. Ibid.

54. See especially Riley, "Our Obligation to the Negro," and Gambrell, "The South's Obligation to the Negroes." See also Victor I. Masters, *The Call of the South* (Atlanta: Publicity Department of the Home Mission Board of the Southern Baptist Convention, 1918), 52–76.

55. August Meier, *Negro Thought in America, 1880–1915, Racial Ideologies in the Age of Booker T. Washington*, Ann Arbor Paperback edition (Ann Arbor: University of Michigan Press, 1973), passim. See especially 69–82 and 130–33. See also Rabinowitz, *Race Relations in the Urban South*, 198–225.

56. Richard Carroll, "Predicts the End of the World," Una Roberts Lawrence Collection, SBHLA, Nashville, Tennessee, box 2, folder 1. This file contains a wealth of information on Carroll. Unfortunately, much of it is excerpted from contemporary newspapers without complete citations. Unless otherwise noted, all material on Carroll from the Una Roberts Lawrence Collection may be assumed to have come from box 2, folder 1.

57. Ibid.

58. See Carroll, "Negro in North Subject of Talk," Una Roberts Lawrence Collection, SBHLA, for a brief statement regarding his mother and slavery.

59. Richard Carroll, "An Appeal to White Christian People," *HF* XXIII (February 1912): 23.

60. Ibid.

61. Ibid.

62. Carroll, "Predicts the End of the World," from *The Yorkville Enquirer*, Una

Roberts Lawrence Collection, SBHLA. This excerpt is not dated, but many similar pieces are dated 1910. The writer noted that Carroll believed this war would occur within twenty-five years. Ironically, America was at war with Japan by the end of 1941.

63. Carroll, as quoted in "Constructive Negro Journalism," *HF* XXIII (November 1911): 19. The article says the incident was taken from *The Southern Ploughman*, September 18, 1911 [?].

64. Ibid.

65. Ibid.

66. Carroll, "Races Should Agree," Una Roberts Lawrence Collection, SBHLA. See also "Richard Carroll's Advice" and "Negro in the North," same collection.

67. Carroll, "Races Should Agree," Una Roberts Lawrence Collection, SBHLA.

68. Carroll, "Negro in North Subject of Talk," Una Roberts Lawrence Collection, SBHLA.

69. Ibid.

70. Carroll, "Men of Character and Worth Needed for the Crisis of the Time," Una Roberts Lawrence Collection, SBHLA.

71. Ibid.

72. See Romans 1:16.

73. Carroll, "The South's Debt to the Negro," May 13, 1915, Una Roberts Lawrence Collection, SBHLA.

74. Ibid.

75. *Aiken Journal and Review*, "Richard Carroll," Una Roberts Lawrence Collection, SBHLA.

76. Editorial, "Constructive Negro Journalism," *HF* XXIII (November 1911): 18.

77. Victor Masters, "Death Silences Voice of Gifted Prophet of Racial Good Will," *The Western Recorder*, November 7, 1929.

78. Ibid.

79. Ibid.

80. William Louis Poteat, "Nat and I," Poteat's Papers, box 9, folder 964, Reynolds Library, Wake Forest University. After the Civil War the Poteats helped Nat (Maurice Nathaniel Corbett) learn to read. In 1908, Poteat said Nat worked for the Federal Government in Washington, D.C.

81. Wheeler, *Uplifting the Race*, xvii.

82. Riley, "Our Obligation to the Negro," 11.

7. Reassessing a Legacy: Southern Baptists Social Christianity, and Regional Context

1. *ESB*, s.v. "Christian Life Commission, The," by A. C. Miller.

2. Ibid. See also McBeth, *The Baptist Heritage*, 656; Baker, *Southern Baptist Convention*, 414–16; and Eighmy, *Churches in Cultural Captivity*, passim.

3. See *ESB*, s.v. "Carnes's Defalcation," by W. W. Barnes; and *ESB*, s.v. "Mountain Mission Schools," by A. B. Cash.

4. Samuel S. Hill, Jr., *The South and the North in American Religion*, Lamar Memorial Lectures, Mercer University, Macon, Georgia, no. 23 (Athens: University of Georgia Press, 1980), 7.

5. Charles Reagan Wilson, *Baptized in Blood: The Religion of the Lost Cause, 1865–1920* (Athens: University of Georgia Press, 1980), 1–17.

6. Ibid.

7. Grantham, *Southern Progressivism*, passim.

8. For reform and Progressive Era reformers see Arthur S. Link and Richard L. McCormick, *Progressivism*, The American History Series, (Arlington Heights: Harlan Davidson, 1983); Nell Irvin Painter, *Standing at Armageddon—The United States, 1877–1919* (New York: W. W. Norton, 1987); and John Milton Cooper, Jr., *Pivotal Decades—The United States, 1900–1920* (New York: W. W. Norton, 1990).

9. See James 1:27.

10. Frederick A. Bode, "Religion and Class Hegemony: A Populist Critique in North Carolina," *Journal of Southern History* 37, no. 3 (August 1971): 417–38.

11. Susan Curtis, *A Consuming Faith—The Social Gospel and Modern American Culture*, New Studies in American Intellectual and Cultural History series, ed. Thomas Bender (Baltimore: Johns Hopkins University Press, 1991), passim.

12. Lois Banner, "Religious Benevolence as Social Control: A Critique of an Interpretation," *Journal of American History* 60 (June 1973): 23–41.

BIBLIOGRAPHY

Primary Sources

General

Isaac Taylor Tichenor's Diary and Miscellaneous Papers, Southern Baptist Theological Seminary, Louisville, Kentucky.

Minutes of The Home Mission Board of The Southern Baptist Convention. 1880–1925.

Minutes of the Boards of Managers, Louisville Baptist Orphans Home, Louisville, Kentucky. 1870–1920.

R. C. Buckner's Papers, Southwestern Baptist Theological Seminary, Fort Worth, Texas.

Southern Baptist Convention. *Annual* of The Southern Baptist Convention. Nashville. 1880–1920.

The Una Roberts Lawrence Collection, Southern Baptist Historical Library and Archives, Nashville, Tennessee.

William Louis Poteat's Papers, Wake Forest University, Winston-Salem, North Carolina.

Southern Baptist Publications (by states)

Alabama. *Annual* of The Alabama Baptist State Convention. Birmingham. 1890–1920.

Arkansas. *Proceedings* of The Arkansas Baptist State Convention. Little Rock. 1890–1920.

Florida. *Annual* of The Florida Baptist Convention. Jacksonville. 1890–1920.

Georgia. *Minutes* of The Baptist Convention of The State of Georgia. Atlanta. 1890–1920.

Kentucky. *Minutes* of The General Association of Baptists in Kentucky. Louisville. 1867–1920.

———. *Minutes* of The Long Run Association. 1867–1920.

Louisiana. *Annual* of The Louisiana Baptist Convention. Shreveport. 1890–1920.

Maryland. *Annual* of The Maryland Baptist Union. Baltimore. 1910–1920.

Mississippi. *Proceedings* of The Mississippi Baptist Convention. Jackson. 1867–1920.

Missouri. *Minutes* of The Missouri Baptist General Association. Jefferson City. 1890–1910.

North Carolina. *Annual* of The North Carolina Baptist State Convention. Raleigh. 1888–1920.

Oklahoma. *Minutes* of The Baptist General Convention of Oklahoma. Oklahoma City. 1900–1915.

South Carolina. *Minutes* of The State Convention of The Baptist Denomination in South Carolina. 1890–1920.

——. *Minutes* of The Spartanburg Association. 1888–1900.

Tennessee. *Annual* of The Tennessee Baptist Convention. Nashville. 1890–1920.

Texas. *Annual* of The Baptist Convention of Texas. Dallas. 1890–1920.

Virginia. *Minutes* of The Baptist General Association of Virginia. Richmond. 1890–1920.

Baptist Newspapers and Periodicals

Alabama Baptist (Birmingham), 1890–1920.

Baptist Courier (Greenville), 1890–1910.

Biblical Recorder (Raleigh), 1887–1920.

The Buckner Orphans Home Annual, 1891–1920.

The Christian Index (Atlanta), 1890–1920.

Home and Foreign Fields.

The Home Field—Also known as *Our Home Field*, 1890–1920.

The Orphan's Friend.

Western Recorder (Louisville), 1870–1920.

Secondary Sources

Ahlstrom, Sydney E. *A Religious History of the American People.* New Haven: Yale University Press, 1972.

An Album of Baptist History in the South. n.p., n.d.

Allen, Catherine B. *A Century to Celebrate: History of Women's Missionary Union.* Birmingham: Women's Missionary Union, 1987.

Alley, Reuben Edward. *A History of Baptists in Virginia.* Richmond: Virginia Baptist General Board, 1973.

Anderson, James D. *The Education of Blacks in the South, 1860–1935.* Chapel Hill: University of North Carolina Press, 1988.

An Educational Study of Alabama. Department of Interior, Bureau of Education Bulletin no. 41, 1919.

Atchison, Ray Morris. *Historical Studies of Alabama Baptist Churches and Associations.* Birmingham: Howard College Library Research Series, paper no. 1 (1958).

Bailey, Hugh C. *Edgar Gardner Murphy—Gentle Progressive.* Coral Gables: University of Miami Press, 1968.

——. *Liberalism in the New South: Southern Social Reformers in the Progressive Movement.* Coral Gables: University of Miami Press, 1969.

Bailey, Kenneth K. *Southern White Protestantism in the Twentieth-Century South.* New York: Harper & Row, 1964.

Baker, Robert A. *Relations Between Northern and Southern Baptists.* 1954. Reprint, New York: Arno Press, 1980.

———. *The Southern Baptist Convention and Its People, 1607–1972.* Nashville: Broadman Press, 1974.

———. *Tell the Generation Following: A History of Southwestern Baptist Theological Seminary, 1908–1983.* Nashville: Broadman Press, 1983.

Banner, Lois. "Religious Benevolence as Social Control: A Critique of an Interpretation." *Journal of American History* 60 (June 1973): 23–41.

Barnes, W. W. *The Southern Baptist Convention, 1845–1953.* Nashville: Broadman Press, 1954.

Barr, Alwyn. *Reconstruction To Reform—Texas Politics, 1876–1906.* Austin: University of Texas Press, 1971.

Berger, Peter L. *The Sacred Canopy.* Garden City: Anchor Books, 1969.

———. *Facing Up to Modernity.* New York: Basic Books, 1977.

Bode, Frederick A. "Religion and Class Hegemony: A Populist Critique in North Carolina." *Journal of Southern History,* 37, no. 3 (August 1971) 417–38.

Boles, John B. "The Discovery of Southern Religious History." In *Interpreting Southern History,* edited by John B. Boles and Evelyn Thomas Nolen, 510–48. Baton Rouge: Louisiana State University Press, 1987.

Boone, Ilsey. *Elements in Baptist Development.* Boston: The Backus Historical Society, 1913.

Boothe, Charles Octavius. *The Cyclopedia of the Colored Baptists of Alabama—Their Leaders and Their Work.* Birmingham: Alabama Publishing, 1895.

Bordin, Ruth Brigitta Anderson. *Women and Temperance: The Quest for Power and Liberty, 1873–1900.* Philadelphia: Temple University Press, 1981.

———. *Francis Willard: A Biography.* Chapel Hill: University of North Carolina Press, 1986.

Brackney, William H. *Baptist Thought and Life, 1600–1980.* Valley Forge: Judson Press, in cooperation with the American Historical Society, 1983.

Braeman, John. *Albert J. Beveridge, American Nationalist.* Chicago: University of Chicago Press, 1971.

Brief History of Spring Meadows. n.p., n.d.

Brooks, Richard Donotto. *One-Hundred and Sixty-Two Years of Middle Tennessee Baptists, 1796–1958.* Nashville: Cullom and Ghertner, 1958.

Brown, A. E. *Southern Baptist Mountain School Work.* Atlanta: Home Mission Board of the Southern Baptist Convention, 1908–9.

———. "Notes from Superintendent Brown." *Our Home Field* XVIII (November 1906).

———. "Mountain Schools." *Our Home Field* XVIII (May 1907).

————. "Mountain School Notes." *Our Home Field* XXII (December 1910).

————. "Our Mountain Schools—Are They Worthwhile?" *The Home Field* XXII (April 1911).

————. "Progress Among the Mountain Schools." *Our Home Field* XXIV (April 1913).

————. "Tact and Love Win a Hardshell Church." *Our Home Field* XXVI (October 1915).

————. "The Mission and Value of Our Mountain Schools." *Home and Foreign Fields* 3 (March 1919).

Brown, C. C. "A Suggested Solution to a Sore Problem." *The Home Field* XXVII (June 1916).

Bruner, James W. *A Guidebook on Baptist Institutions in Texas.* Dallas: Harben-Spotts, 1941.

Bruner, Weston. "Southern Baptists and Negro Baptists." *The Home Field* XXIV (December 1913).

Buck, John T. *History of the Mississippi Baptist State Convention.* Jackson: Charles Winkley, 1883.

Burrows, Lansing. *Tichenor Memorial of the Church Building Loan Fund.* Baltimore: Women's Missionary Union, 1903.

Burton, Joe W. *Epochs of Home Missions.* Atlanta: Home Mission Board, 1945.

Buswell, James O., III. *Slavery, Segregation and Scripture.* Grand Rapids: William B. Eerdmans Publishing, 1964.

Carroll, Benajah Harvey. *An Interpretation of the English Bible.* 6 vols. Grand Rapids: Baker Book House, 1976.

Carroll, James Milton. *A History of Texas Baptists.* Dallas: Baptist Standard, 1923.

Carroll, Richard. "An Appeal to White Christian People." *The Home Field* XXIII (February 1912).

Cartwright, Joseph H. *The Triumph of Jim Crow.* Knoxville: University of Tennessee Press, 1976.

Christian, John T. *A History of the Baptists of Louisiana.* Shreveport: The Executive Board of the Louisiana Baptist Convention, 1923.

Clement, Priscilla Ferguson. "Families and Foster Care: Philadelphia in the Late Nineteenth Century." In *Growing Up in America*, edited by N. Ray Hiner and Joseph M. Hawes, 135–46. Urbana: University of Illinois Press, 1985.

Commons, John R. *Social Reform and the Church.* New York: Thomas Y. Crowell, 1894. Reprint in the Reprints of Economic Classics Series, New York: Augustus M. Kelley Publishers, 1967.

Cooper, John Milton, Jr. *Pivitol Decades—The United States, 1900–1920*, New York: W. W. Norton, 1990.

Cranfill, J. B., and J. L. Walker. *R. C. Buckner's Life of Faith and Works.*

1914. Reprinted and enlarged, Dallas: Buckner's Orphans Home, 1916.

Crews, Mickey. *The Church of God—A Social History.* Knoxville: University of Tennessee Press, 1990.

Curtis, Susan. *A Consuming Faith—The Social Gospel and Modern American Culture.* New Studies in American Intellectual and Cultural History series, edited by Thomas Bender. Baltimore: Johns Hopkins University Press, 1991.

Dabney, Charles William. *Universal Education in the South.* 2 vols. Chapel Hill: University of North Carolina Press, 1936.

Davidson, Elizabeth H. *Child Labor Legislation in the Southern Textile States.* Chapel Hill: University of North Carolina Press, 1939.

Davis, David Brion. *Antebellum American Culture.* Lexington, Mass.: D. C. Heath, 1979.

Dawley, Thomas Robinson, Jr. *The Child That Toileth Not.* New York: Garcia Publishing, 1912.

Degler, Carl N. *The Other South.* New York: Harper & Row, 1974.

———. *At Odds.* New York: Oxford University Press, 1980.

Dill, J. S. "Missions in the Southern States." Pamphlet published by The Maryland Baptist Mission Rooms, October 1894.

———. *Isaac Taylor Tichenor.* Nashville: Sunday School Board of the Southern Baptist Convention, 1908.

Douglas, Harlan Paul. *Christian Reconstruction in the South.* Boston: The Pilgrim Press, 1909.

Douglas, J. D., general ed. *New Twentieth-Century Encyclopedia of Religious Knowledge.* 2d ed. Grand Rapids: Baker Book House, 1991.

Douglas, Robert Sidney. *History of Missouri Baptists.* Kansas City: Western Baptist Publishing, 1934.

Dunn, Loula. *The Story of the Alabama Children's Home.* Montgomery: Paragon Press, 1945.

Durham, Columbus. "Letter." In *The Biblical Recorder.* July 30, 1884.

Durham, James W. "The Christianization of the South." *The Home Field* XXIII (February 1912).

Eager, George Broadman. *Lectures in Ecclesiology.* Louisville: Mayes Printing, 1917.

"Editorial." *Our Home Field* XVIII (October 1906).

———. *Our Home Field* XVIII (January 1907).

———. *Our Home Field* XVIII (March 1907).

———. *The Home Field* XXII (September 1910).

———. "Constructive Negro Journalism." *The Home Field* XXIII (November 1911).

———. *The Home Field* XXV (January 1914).

Edmunds, Richard H. "Baptist Opportunity in the Growing South." *Our Home Field* XXI (June 1910).

————. "The Pulpit and Sociology." *The Home Field* XXIII (February 1912).

Eighmy, John Lee. *Churches in Cultural Captivity: A History of the Social Attitudes of Southern Baptists.* 1972. Reprint, with revised introduction, conclusion, and bibliography by Samuel S. Hill, Knoxville: University of Tennessee Press, 1987.

Eller, Ronald D. *Miners, Millhands, and Mountaineers: Industrialization of the Appalachian South, 1880–1930.* Knoxville: University of Tennessee Press, 1982.

Ellis, William E. *"A Man of Books and a Man of the People:" E. Y. Mullins and the Crisis of Moderate Baptist Leadership.* Macon: Mercer University Press, 1985.

Encyclopedia of Southern Baptists. Nashville: Broadman Press, 1958. S.v. "Carnes's Defalcation," by W. W. Barnes.

————. S.v. "Primitive Baptists," by W. J. Berry.

————. S.v. "Mountain Mission Schools," by A. B. Cash.

————. S.v. "Mississippi Baptist Orphanage," by W. C. Cathey.

————. S.v. "Gardner, Charles Spurgeon," by Leo T. Crismon.

————. S.v. "Southern Baptist Theological Seminary," by Leo T. Crismon.

————. S.v. "Eager, George Broadman," by Gaines S. Dobbins.

————. S.v. "Bruner, Weston," by John F. Havlik.

————. S.v. "Tichenor, Isaac Taylor," by Kimball Johnson.

————. S.v. "Riley, Benjamin Franklin," by Terry L. Jones.

————. S.v. "Brown, Clinton Capers," by William R. McLin.

————. S.v. "Christian Life Commission, The," by A. C. Miller.

————. S.v. "Church," by Theron D. Price.

————. S.v. "Negroes, Southern Baptist Relations to," by Courts Redford.

————. S.v. "Association, The District," by E. C. Routh.

————. S.v. "Convention, The State," by E. C. Routh.

————. S.v. "Carroll, Benajah Harvey," by Franklin M. Segler.

————. S.v. "Southern Baptist Convention," by J. W. Storer.

————. S.v. "Boyce, James Petigru," by Hugh Wamble.

————. S.v. "Brown, Albert Erskine," by W. H. Williams.

Flynt, Wayne. "The Negro and Alabama Baptists During the Progessive Era." *The Journal of the Alabama Academy of Science* 39 (April 1968): 163–67.

————. "Dissent in Zion: Alabama Baptists and Social Issues, 1900–1914." *Journal of Southern History* 35 (winter 1969): 523–42.

————. "Southern Baptists and Reform: 1890–1920." *Baptist History and Heritage* 7 (October 1972): 211–22.

————. *Dixie's Forgotten People.* Bloomington: Indiana University Press, 1979.

——. "The Impact of Social Factors on Southern Baptist Expansion, 1800–1914." *Baptist History and Heritage* 17 (July 1982): 20–31.

——. *Poor but Proud: Alabama's Poor Whites.* Tuscaloosa: University of Alabama Press, 1989.

——. " 'Feeding the Hungry and Ministering to the Broken Hearted': The Presbyterian Church in the United States and the Social Gospel, 1900–1920." In *Religion in the South,* edited by Charles Reagan Wilson, 83–137. The Chancellor's Symposium series. Jackson: University Press of Mississippi, 1985.

Foner, Eric. *Reconstruction—America's Unfinished Revolution.* The New American Nation series. New York: Harper & Row, 1988.

Frazier, E. Franklin, and C. Eric Lincoln. *The Negro Church in America/The Black Church Since Frazier.* New York: Schocken Books, 1974.

Gambrell, J. B. "The South's Obligation to the Negroes." *The Home Field* XXII (September 1910).

Gardner, Charles Spurgeon. "Home Missions and Social Improvement." *Our Home Field* XXI (November 1909).

——. *The Ethics of Jesus and Social Progress.* New York: George H. Doran, 1914.

Gaskin, J. M. *Baptist Milestones in Oklahoma.* Printed by Good Printing Company (no city). N.p., 1966.

——. *Baptist Women in Oklahoma.* Oklahoma City: Messenger Press, 1985.

——. *The McConnell Years in Oklahoma.* Oklahoma City: Messenger Press, 1989.

Gaston, Paul M. *The New South Creed: A Study in Southern Mythmaking.* New York: Alfred A. Knopf, 1970.

Geertz, Clifford. "Religion as a Cultural System." In *The Religious Situation: 1968,* edited by Donald R. Cutler, 639–87. Boston: Beacon Press, 1968.

General Education Board, The. *Report of the Secretary, 1914–1915.* New York: The General Education Board, 1915.

Genovese, Eugene D. *Roll, Jordan, Roll.* New York: Pantheon Books, 1972.

Goodwyn, Lawrence. *Democratic Promise: The Populist Movement in America.* New York: Oxford University Press, 1976.

——. *The Populist Moment.* New York: Oxford University Press, 1978.

Gore, D. L. "The Negro Race." *The Home Field* XXII (July 1911).

Grantham, Dewey W. "The Contours of Southern Progressivism." *American Historical Review* 86 (December 1981): 1035–59.

——. *Southern Progressivism: The Reconciliation of Tradition and Progress.* Twentieth-Century America series. Knoxville: University of Tennessee Press, 1983.

Griffin, Charles Milton. *The Story of North Carolina Baptists, 1683–1933.* Greenwood: Presses of Connie Maxwell Orphanage, 1934.

Gwaltney, Leslie Lee. *Forty of the Twentieth.* Birmingham: n.p., 1940.

Hall, Jacquelyn Dowd. *Revolt Against Chivalry: Jesse Daniel Ames and the Women's Campaign Against Lynching.* New York: Columbia University Press, 1979.

Handy, Robert T., ed. *The Social Gospel in America.* New York: Oxford University Press, 1966.

Hardaway, Grace Lewis. *A History of the Louisville Baptist Orphans Home.* N.p., n.d.

Hart, Roger L. *Redeemers, Bourbons and Populists—Tennessee, 1870–1896.* Baton Rouge: Louisiana State University Press, 1975.

Hartford, Ellis Ford. *The Little White Schoolhouse.* Kentucky Bicentennial Bookshelf Series. Lexington: University of Kentucky Press, 1977.

Hatcher, William Eldridge. *Essays and Addresses Presented at the Second Congress of Virginia Baptists.* Baltimore: H. M. Wharton, 1886.

Hemmingway, Theodore. "Richard Carroll: A Portrait of a Black Leader." *Negro History* bulletin 42 (January–March 1979): 12–13.

Hicks, John D. *The Populist Revolt: A History of the Farmers' Alliance and the People's Party.* N.p.: University of Minnesota Press, 1931. Reprint, Lincoln: University of Nebraska Press—A Bison Book, 1961.

Hill, Samuel S., Jr. *Southern Churches in Crisis.* New York: Holt, Rinehart & Winston, 1966.

——. *The South and the North in American Religion.* Lamar Memorial Lectures, Mercer University, Macon, Georgia, no. 23. Athens: University of Georgia Press, 1980.

——, ed. *Religion in the Solid South.* Nashville: Abingdon Press, 1972.

Hinson, E. Glenn. *A History of Baptists in Arkansas.* Little Rock: Arkansas Baptist State Convention, 1979.

A Historical Summary of State Services for Children in Alabama. United States Department of Labor, bureau publication no. 239, pt. 3 (1938).

History of the Baptist Home for Children. N.p., May 20, 1990.

Hollingsworth, Mary A. "Adopting Children." *The Orphan's Friend* 1 (February 1872).

——. "Education." *The Orphan's Friend* 1 (March 1872).

——. "An Amusing Incident." *The Orphan's Friend* 1 (April 1872).

——. "Our Infirmary." *The Orphan's Friend* 2 (May 1873).

Holly, Alonzo Potter Burgess. *God and the Negro.* Nashville: National Baptist Publishing Board, 1937.

Holt, Andrew David. *The Struggle for a State System of Public Schools in Tennessee, 1903–1936.* Teachers College, Columbia University Contributions to Education, no. 753. New York: Bureau of Publications, Teachers College, Columbia University, 1938.

Home Mission Board of the Southern Baptist Convention, *Annual Leaflet.* Baltimore: Baptist Mission Rooms, 1899.

Hooker, Elizabeth R. *Religion in the Highlands*. With a section on Missionary and Philanthropic Schools by Fannie W. Dunn. New York: The Polygraphic Company of America, 1933.

Hopkins, C. Howard. *The Rise of the Social Gospel in American Protestantism, 1865–1915*. New Haven: Yale University Press, 1940.

Horton, H. D. *A History of the Ozark Division Mountain Schools of the Home Mission Board Southern Baptist Convention*. N.p., 1958.

Hudson, Winthrop S. *Religion in America*. 2d ed. New York: Charles Scribner's Sons, 1973.

Huggins, Maldy Alton. *A History of North Carolina Baptists, 1727–1932*. Raleigh: The General Board, Baptist State Convention of North Carolina, 1967.

Hunter, James Davidson. *American Evangelicals*. New Brunswick: Rutgers University Press, 1983.

———. *Evangelicalism—The Coming Generation*. Chicago: University of Chicago Press, 1987.

Jamison, A. T. *Your Boy and Girl*. Nashville: Sunday School Board of the Southern Baptist Convention, 1922.

———. *The Institution for Children*. Columbia, S.C.: Baptist Book Depository, 1926 [?].

———. *Forty Years of Connie Maxwell History*. Greenwood: Board of Trustees, Connie Maxwell Orphanage, 1932.

———. *Consider the Parasite*. Columbia, S.C.: Baptist Book Depository, n.d.

Joiner, Edward Earl. *A History of the Florida Baptists*. Jacksonville: Convention Press, 1972.

Jones, William R. *Is God a White Racist?* C. Eric Lincoln Series on Black Religion. Garden City: Anchor Press, 1973.

Keith-Lucas, Alan. *A History of Connie Maxwell Children's Home, 1892–1977*. Greenwood: Connie Maxwell Children's Home, 1982.

———. *A Hundred Years of Caring*. Thomasville, N.C.: Baptist Children's Homes of North Carolina, 1985.

Kelsey, George D. *Social Ethics Among Southern Baptists, 1917–1969*. Atla Monograph Series, no. 2. Metuchen: Scarecrow Press and American Theological Library Association, 1973.

Kendall, William Frederick. *A History of the Tennessee Baptist Convention*. Brentwood, Tenn.: Executive Board of the Tennessee Baptist Convention, 1974.

Kett, Joseph F. *Rites of Passage*. New York: Basic Books, 1977.

King, Joe Madison. *A History of South Carolina Baptists*. Columbia, S.C.: General Board of the South Carolina Baptist Convention, 1964.

King, William McGuire. "The Biblical Base of the Social Gospel." In *The Bible and Social Reform*, edited by Ernest R. Sandeen, 59–84. Philadelphia: Fortress Press, 1982.

Leavell, Zachary Taylor. *A Complete History of Mississippi Baptists, from the Earliest Times.* 2 vols. Jackson: Mississippi Baptist Publishing, 1904.

Leonard, Bill J. *God's Last and Only Hope.* Grand Rapids: William B. Eerdmans Publishing, 1990.

Lincoln, C. Eric. *Race, Religion and the Continuing American Dilemma.* New York: Hill and Wang, 1984.

Linder, Robert D. "The Resurgency of Evangelical Social Concern (1925–1975)." In *The Evangelicals,* edited by David F. Wells and John D. Woodbridge, 177–215. Nashville: Abingdon Press, 1975. Reprint, Grand Rapids: Baker Book House, 1977.

Linder, Suzanne Cameron. *William Louis Poteat—Prophet of Progress.* Chapel Hill: University of North Carolina Press, 1966.

Link, Arthur S. "The Progressive Movement in the South, 1870–1914." *North Carolina Historical Review* 23 (April 1946): 172–95.

Link, Arthur S., and Richard L. McCormick. *Progressivism.* Arlington Heights: Harlan Davidson, 1983.

Lippy, Charles H. *Bibliography of Religion in the South.* Macon: Mercer University Press, 1985.

LuBove, Roy. *The Professional Altruist: The Emergence of Social Work as a Career, 1880–1930.* A publication of the Center for the Study of the History of Liberty in America. Cambridge: Harvard University Press, 1965.

Lumpkin, William L. *Baptist Confessions of Faith.* Revised ed., 1969. Reprint, Valley Forge: Judson Press, 1980.

Marsden, George M. *Fundamentalism and American Culture.* New York: Oxford University Press, 1980.

———. *Religion and American Culture.* San Diego: Harcourt Brace Jovanovich, 1990.

———. *Understanding Fundamentalism and Evangelicalism.* Grand Rapids: William B. Eerdmans Publishing, 1991.

Masters, Victor I. "The Mountain People." *Our Home Field* XX (April 1909).

———. "The Church and Social Unrest." *The Home Field* XXIII (January 1912).

———. *The Home Mission Task.* Atlanta: Blosser, 1912.

———. *Baptist Missions in the South.* 3d ed. Atlanta: Publicity Department of the Home Mission Board of the Southern Baptist Convention, 1915.

———. *The Call of the South.* Atlanta: Publicity Department of the Home Mission Board of the Southern Baptist Convention, 1918.

Matthews, Donald G. *Religion in the Old South.* Chicago History of American Religion Series, edited by Martin E. Marty. Chicago: University of Chicago Press, 1977.

———. "The Second Great Awakening as an Organizing Process, 1780–1830: An Hypothesis." *American Quarterly* 21 (spring 1969): 23–43.

May, Henry F. *Protestant Churches in Industrial America.* New York: Harper & Brothers, 1949.

McBeth, H. Leon. *The Baptist Heritage: Four Centuries of Baptist Witness.* Nashville: Broadman Press, 1987.

McDowell, John Patrick. *The Social Gospel in the South: The Women's Home Mission Movement in the Methodist Episcopal Church, South, 1886–1939.* Baton Rouge: Louisiana State University Press, 1982.

McGlothlin, William J. "The Seminary and Mountain and Frontier Missions." *Our Home Field* XXI (October 1909).

McLemore, Richard Aubrey. *A History of Mississippi Baptists, 1780–1970.* Jackson: Mississippi Baptist Convention Board, 1971.

McLeod, John Angus. *From These Stones—Mars Hill College, 1856–1967.* 1955. Revised ed., Mars Hill, N.C.: Mars Hill College, 1968.

McMath, Robert C., Jr. *Populist Vanguard: A History of the Southern Farmers' Alliance.* Chapel Hill: University of North Carolina Press, 1975. Reprint, New York: W. W. Norton, 1977.

McPherson, James M. "White Liberals and Black Power in Negro Education, 1865–1915." *American Historical Review* 75 (June 1970): 1357–86.

Mead, Frank S. *Handbook of Denominations in the United States.* 6th ed. Nashville: Abingdon Press, 1975.

Mead, Sidney E. *The Lively Experiment: The Shaping of Christianity in America.* 1963. Paperback ed., New York: Harper & Row, 1976.

Meier, August. *Negro Thought in America, 1880–1915, Racial Ideologies in the Age of Booker T. Washington.* Ann Arbor paperback edition. Ann Arbor: University of Michigan Press, 1973.

Melton, J. Gordon, ed. *The Encyclopedia of American Religions.* 3d ed. Detroit: Gale Research, 1989.

Minus, Paul M. *Walter Rauschenbusch: American Reformer.* New York: Macmillan, 1988.

Morris, E. C. "Dr. C. C. Brown and the Negro." *The Home Field* XXVII (June 1916).

Mullins, E. Y. "The Crisis in Home Missions." *Our Home Field* XVIII (January 1907).

O'Hara, Joel William. *Signal Fires on the Mountains.* Nashville: The Sunday School Board of the Southern Baptist Convention, 1929.

Painter, Nell Irvin. *Standing at Armageddon—The United States, 1877–1919.* New York: W. W. Norton, 1987.

Pelt, Owen D., and Ralph Lee Smith. *The Story of the National Baptists.* New York: Vantage Press, 1960.

Platt, Anthony M. *The Child Savers.* 2d ed., Chicago: University of Chicago Press, 1977.

Pope, Liston. *Millhands and Preachers.* New Haven: Yale University Press, 1942.

Poteat, William Louis. "Christianity and Society." In *The Biblical Recorder.* August 16, 1905.

Price, J. M. *Christianity and Social Problems*. Nashville: Sunday School Board of the Southern Baptist Convention, 1928.

Pugh, Thomas E. *As a Grain of Mustard Seed*. Roanoke: Progress Press, 1983.

Pulley, Raymond H. *Old Virginia Restored*. Charlottesville: University Press of Virginia, 1968.

Rabinowitz, Howard N. *Race Relations in the Urban South, 1865–1890*. Foreword by C. Vann Woodward. Blacks in the New World series, edited by August Meier. New York: Oxford University Press, 1978. Reprint, Illini Books edition, Urbana: University of Illinois Press, 1980.

Ragsdale, Barton Davis. *Story of the Georgia Baptists* (3 vols.). Published by the author under the auspices of the Executive Committee of the Georgia Baptist Convention. Printed by Foote and Davies, 1932.

Ransom, Roger L., and Richard Sutch. *One Kind of Freedom*. Cambridge: Cambridge University Press, 1977.

Reed, Weston C. *Love in Action—The Story of the Baptist Children's Homes of North Carolina*. Thomasville, N.C.: Baptist Children's Homes of North Carolina, 1973.

Richardson, Joe M. *Christian Reconstruction*. Athens: University of Georgia Press, 1986.

Riley, B. F. "Our Obligation to the Negro." *The Home Field* XXII (September 1910).

Robertson, Archibald Thomas, ed. *Life and Letters of John Albert Broadus*. Philadelphia: American Baptist Publication Society, 1901.

Rosenberg, Ellen M. *The Southern Baptists: A Subculture in Transition*. Knoxville: University of Tennessee Press, 1989.

Rothman, David J. *The Discovery of the Asylum*. Boston: Little, Brown, 1971.

———. *Conscience and Convenience*. Boston: Little, Brown, 1980.

Routh, Eugene Coke. *The Story of Oklahoma Baptists*. Oklahoma City: Baptist General Convention, 1932.

Ryland, Garnett. *The Baptists of Virginia, 1699–1926*. Richmond: Virginia Baptist Board of Missions and Education, 1955.

St. Amant, C. Penrose. *A Short History of Louisiana Baptists*. Nashville: Broadman Press, 1948.

Sandeen, Ernest R., ed. *The Bible and Social Reform*. Philadelphia: Fortress Press, 1982.

Scott, Anne F. "Women, Religion, and Social Change in the South, 1830–1930." In *Religion in the Solid South*, edited by Samuel S. Hill, Jr., 92–121. Nashville: Abingdon Press, 1972.

Sellers, James Benson. *The Prohibition Movement in Alabama, 1707 to 1943*. Chapel Hill: University of North Carolina Press, 1943.

Shapiro, Henry D. *Appalachia on Our Mind: The Southern Mountains and Mountaineers in the American Conscience, 1870–1920*. Chapel Hill: University of North Carolina Press, 1978.

Smith, H. Sheldon. *In His Image, But* . . . . Durham: Duke University Press, 1972.

Smith, Timothy L. *Revivalism and Social Reform: American Protestantism on the Eve of the Civil War.* Nashville: Abingdon Press, 1957.

Speer, Robert E. *Race and Race Relations.* New York: Fleming H. Revell, 1924.

Spain, Rufus B. *At Ease in Zion: A Social History of Southern Baptists, 1865–1900.* Nashville: Vanderbilt University Press, 1967.

Spilman, Bernard Washington. *The Mills Home.* Printed by the Mills Home, Thomasville, N.C., 1932.

Storey, John W. *Texas Baptist Leadership and Social Christianity, 1900–1980.* College Station: Texas A&M Press, 1986.

Thompson, James J., Jr. *Tried as by Fire: Southern Baptists and the Religious Controversies of the 1920s.* Macon: Mercer University Press, 1982.

Tindall, George Brown. "Business Progressivism: Southern Politics in the Twenties." *The South Atlantic Quarterly* 62 (1963): 93–106.

————. *The Emergence of the New South, 1913–1945.* Vol. 10. The History of the South Series, edited by Wendell Holmes Stephenson and E. Merton Coulter. 1967. Paperback reprint, Baton Rouge: Louisiana State University Press, 1983.

————. *The Persistent Tradition in New South Politics.* The Walter Lynwood Fleming Lectures in Southern History Series. Baton Rouge: Louisiana State University Press, 1975.

————. *The Ethnic Southerners.* Baton Rouge: Louisiana State University Press, 1976.

Tull, James E. *Shapers of Baptist Thought.* Valley Forge: Judson Press, 1972.

Walker, Anne Kendrick. *The Story of the Alabama Baptist Childrens Home.* In Collaboration with James O. Colley, Sr. Montgomery: The Paragon Press, 1945.

Warrenton (signed letter). *The Biblical Recorder.* July 16, 1884.

Washington, Booker T. *The Future of the American Negro.* New York: Haskell House, 1968.

Washington, Booker T., and W. E. Burghardt DuBose. *The Negro in the South.* The William Levi Bull Lectures for 1907. Philadelphia: George W. Jacobs, 1907.

Watson, Frank Dekker. *The Charity Organization Movement in the United States.* New York: Macmillan, 1922.

Weatherford, W. D., ed. *Religion in the Appalachian Mountains—A Symposium.* Berea, Ky.: Berea College, 1955.

Weatherford, W. D., and Earl D. C. Brewer. *Life and Religion in Southern Appalachia.* New York: Friendship Press, 1962.

Weeks, Stephen B. *History of Public School Education in Alabama.* Bulletin no. 12, whole no. 637. Washington, D.C.: Government Printing Office, 1915.

Wells, David F., and John D. Woodbridge, eds. *The Evangelicals.* Nashville: Abingdon Press, 1975. Reprint, Grand Rapids: Baker Book House, 1977.

Wheeler, Edward L. *Uplifting the Race.* Lanham, Md.: University Press of America, 1986.

White, John E. "The Southern Mountaineer." *Our Home Field* XXI (August 1909).

———. "Ten Years of Partnership." *Our Home Field* XXI (October 1909).

White, Ronald C., Jr., and C. Howard Hopkins. *The Social Gospel—Religion and Reform in a Changing America.* Philadelphia: Temple University Press, 1976.

Williamson, Joel. *The Crucible of Race: Black-White Relations in the American South since Emancipation.* New York: Oxford University Press, 1984.

———. *A Rage for Order: Black-White Relations in the American South Since Emancipation.* New York: Oxford University Press, 1986.

Wilson, Charles Reagan. *Baptized in Blood: The Religion of the Lost Cause, 1865–1920.* Athens: University of Georgia Press, 1980.

———, ed. *Religion in the South.* Jackson: University Press of Mississippi, 1985.

Wilson, Samuel Tyndale. *The Southern Mountaineers.* New York: Literature Department, Presbyterian Home Missions, 1906.

Wisner, Elizabeth. *Social Welfare in the South.* Baton Rouge: Louisiana State University Press, 1970.

Wood, Forrest G. *The Arrogance of Faith: Christianity and Race in America from the Colonial Era to the Twentieth Century.* New York: Alfred A. Knopf, 1990.

Woodson, Carter G. and Wesley, Charles H. *The Negro in Our History.* 10th ed. Washington, D.C.: Associated Publishers, 1962.

Woodward, C. Vann. *Origins of the New South, 1877–1913.* Baton Rouge: Louisiana State University Press, 1951.

Zelizer, Viviana A. *Pricing the Priceless Child.* New York: Basic Books, 1985.

Unpublished Sources

Beavers, Theresa Aguglia. "The Italians of the Birmingham District." M.A. thesis, Samford University, 1969.

Brennan, James A., III. "Legislation for the Working Children of Alabama: Growth and Reform of the Cotton Textile Mills to 1903." M.A. thesis, Samford University, 1971.

Brimm, Hugh A. "The Social Consciousness of Southern Baptists in Relation to Some Regional Problems, 1910–1935." Th.D. dissertation, Southern Baptist Theological Seminary, 1944.

Burrows, John Howard. "The Great Disturber: The Social Philosophy and

Theology of Alfred James Dickinson." M.A. thesis, Samford University, 1971.

Crider, Robert F. "The Social Philosophy of L. L. Gwaltney, 1919–1950." M.A. thesis, Samford University, 1969.

Cruse, Irma Russell. "Hardin Edwards Taliaferro: Baptist Preacher-Editor, 1811–1875." M.A. thesis, Samford University, 1984.

Davison, Charles Clement. "Race Friction in the South Since 1865." Th.D. dissertation, Southern Baptist Theological Seminary, 1922.

Dunn, James M. "The Ethical Thought of Joseph Martin Dawson." Th.D. dissertation, Southwestern Baptist Theological Seminary, 1966.

Hughes, John Edward. "A History of the Southern Baptist Convention's Ministry to the Negro, 1845–1904." Th.D. dissertation, Southern Baptist Theological Seminary, 1971.

Jones, Terry Lawrence. "Attitudes of Alabama Baptists Toward Negroes, 1890–1914." M.A. thesis, Samford University, 1968.

May, Lynn E. "Southern Baptist Social Consciousness, 1845–1855." M.A. thesis, Vanderbilt University, 1968.

Melvin, Robert. "The Life and Thought of Walter Nathan Johnson." Doctor of Divinity thesis, Vanderbilt University, Divinity School, 1975.

Roberts, Anthony Dale. "Jesse Burton Witherspoon: The Ethics of Advocacy in a Southern Baptist Context." Ph.D. dissertation, Southern Baptist Theological Seminary, 1983.

Robinson, William Elijah. "The Eldridge (Alabama) Baptist Academy." M.A. Ed. thesis, University of Alabama, 1947.

Sisk, Willie Kyle. "The Attitude of the White Race Toward the Negro." Th.D. dissertation, Southern Baptist Theological Seminary, 1923.

West, Walter. "Samuel Lewis Morgan and the Social Gospel Movement— A Southern Baptist Pastor's Experience with Social Christianity, 1910–1922." Unpublished essay in Wake Forrest University's Baptist Collect.

INDEX

Acree, R. R., 24–25
African Americans, 89, 91–92, 103, 110
Aiken Journal and Review, 108
Alliance (agricultural), 16–17
Allison, Osie, 78, 84–85
Appalachia, 7, 72–88. *See also* Mountain Mission Schools

Bailey, Kenneth K., 3, 29
Baker, Robert A., 15
Baptist Standard, 8, 100
Beecher, Catherine, 70
Bible, 3, 7, 11, 14, 20, 29, 36, 38, 64, 77, 80, 97, 104–5, 117
Biblical Recorder, 50
Blacks: rights of, 7; Baptist attitudes toward lynching of, 30; teacher salaries of, 74–75; white attitudes toward, 88–91; education of, 92–103; Richard Carroll's attitude toward, 104–8; Baptist attitude toward, 117–19
Boles, John B., 6, 8, 10
Boyce, James Petigru, 29
Broadus, John A., 30, 37
Brown, Albert E., 23–25, 77–79, 81–84, 86–88
Brown, C. C., 99, 101–2
Bruner, Weston, 102
Buckner, Robert Cooke, 37, 51–52, 55, 57–58, 60–61, 69
Buswell, James O. III, 98

Carnes, C. S., 113
Carroll, Benajah Harvey, 34–37
Carroll, Richard, 104–9, 117
Child, Lydia, 70
Choat, Christopher Columbus, 81
Christian Life Commission, 112
Civil War, 15–16, 20, 29, 36–37, 42, 48–51, 53, 73, 91, 98, 105, 114

Clement, Priscilla Ferguson, 66
Congregationalists, 2
Connie Maxwell Home, 55, 57–59, 63–64, 68–69
Corbitt, Charles Linwood, 59
Crop lien, 16–17, 20
Cultural captivity, 4–5, 12, 113–15, 118
Culture, 1, 5, 13–18, 20–21, 27, 59, 88, 97, 110, 114, 116

Dabney, William, 75
Daws, S. O., 17
Drennen, Oscar M., 84
Durham, Columbus, 50–51

Eager, George Broadman, 33–34
Eaton, T. T., 94
Edmunds, Richard H., 44–46, 89
Education, 7, 14, 17–20, 23, 28–29, 36–37, 42, 61–64, 67–68, 70, 72–77, 79–85, 87–88, 90, 95–99, 102, 107–8, 110, 112–13, 116, 119
Eighmy, John Lee, 4–5, 7, 8, 12
Elbridge Baptist Academy, 75
Ely, Richard T., 2
Episcopalians, 2
Ethics, 16, 22, 25, 31–32, 46, 116, 118
Evangelism, 11, 13–14, 16, 20, 23–24, 44, 47, 53, 70, 100, 102, 113–14, 118

Family, 8, 12, 14, 24–25, 32–34, 59–61, 66–68, 87, 112, 115–18
Feuding, 23
Fleming, R. D., 51
Flynt, J. Wayne, 6–10
Foner, Eric, 91
Fortress Monroe Conference, 92, 94–95, 100

Gambrell, J. B., 100, 102
Gardner, Charles Spurgeon, 23, 25, 30–33, 37
Georgia, 7; Baptist orphanage in, 53–64; mountain schools in, 76, 79; race relations in, 96
Gladden, Washington, 2, 9
Golden, W. C., 56
Goodwyn, Lawrence, 16–18
Gore, D. L., 98
Greene, George W., 51
Gwaltney, W. R., 51

Handy, Robert T., 2, 9
Hardaway, Grace Lewis, 49
Hardshell Baptists, 82
Harrison-Chilaowee Institute, 84, 123
Hiawasee Institute, 76, 122
Hill, Samuel S., Jr., 5–6, 8, 10, 113
Home Mission Board, 13–14, 21, 28, 38, 43, 46, 53; and mountain schools, 74, 76–82, 87; and race relations, 87, 92, 97, 102, 108
Home Mission Society, 92–97, 100
Hopkins, Charles Howard, 1–2, 10
Hufham, J. D., 51

Illiteracy, 75
Immigrants: mission work and assimilation of, 21–24, 44, 47; and Northern Baptist work, 94–95; and southern blacks, 101
Industrialization: and rise of Social Gospel, 1–15; and opportunity for Baptist mission work, 31–32; South's need for, 43–44; no sustained critique of, 118

Jamison, A. T., 55, 59, 62–63, 67–69
Jones, C. A., 81

Lamb, William, 17
Leonard, Bill J., 20
Linder, Robert D., 11
Lingle, Walter L., 7
Lorimer, George C., 49–50
Lost Causism, 114
Louise Short Widows and Orphans Home, 55

Louisville Baptist Orphans Home, 49, 52, 58, 62, 64–65

Masters, Victor, 46, 87, 108–9
Mathews, Donald G., 13
May, Henry F., 1–2, 9
McBeth, H. Leon, 15, 93–94
McGlothlin, William J., 22–23
McManaway, A. G., 51
Mead, Sidney E., 9–10
Meier, August, 103
Methodist Episcopal Church, South, 6
Methodists, 2–3, 6
Mills, John Haymes, 50–51, 62, 64, 69
Mills Home, 51–52, 62, 64
Morehouse, Henry, 93
Morris, E. C., 102
Mother's Book, The, 70
Mountain Mission Schools, 11, 23–26, 44, 72–79, 81–89, 112–13, 117
Movement culture, 16–18; self-awareness as a feature of, 53
Mullins, E. Y., 20–21

National Baptist Convention, 97, 102
Negro Baptist Education Society, 96
New Era Institutes, 97. See also Appendix II
North Carolina: Baptist orphanage in, 50–69; mountain schools of, 75–88; race relations in, 96, 98. See also Mills Home
Norton, William F., 58

Organic society, 12, 90, 115–17
Overby, R. R., 51
Ozark Mountains, 72, 79

Paternalism, 87, 100, 116
Patriotism, 23–24, 33, 36
Place, sense of, 12, 90, 99, 107
Populism, 12–13, 16–18, 27
Poteat, William Louis, 22, 109
Presbyterians, 2–3, 6–7, 76, 81, 84
Progressivism, 28, 31, 88

Race relations, 8, 14, 89, 91, 100, 103–4, 106, 111–12
Ramey, D. A., 81

Rauschenbusch, Walter, 2, 7
Religious Messenger, The, 51
Riley, B. F., 101, 110–11
Rothman, David J., 65–67, 70
Routh, E. C., 19

Scarborough, John C., 51
Scroggins, T. S., 64
Shapiro, Henry D., 73
Sharecropping, 20
Social Christianity, 1–8; defined, 11–12; and cultural context, 16–25; and missionary activity, 47; and child care, 48–71; and race relations, 103, 108, 112–15
Social Gospel, 1–11, 113
Socialism, 22–24
South Carolina. *See* Connie Maxwell Home
Southern Baptist Theological Seminary, 20, 22, 29–34
Southwestern Baptist Theological Seminary, 20, 29, 34–36
Spain, Rufus, 3–4, 8
Stockton's Valley Institute, 81, 123
Storey, John W., 7–8, 10–11

Taylor, Charles E., 51
Tennessee: Baptist orphanage in, 56, 61, 63; education in, 74; mountain schools in, 77, 79–80
Texas Baptist, The, 52
Thompson, James J., Jr., 5
Tichenor, Isaac Taylor, 37–45, 76, 94
Treatise on Domestic Economy for Young Ladies at Home, A, 70

Uplift: for white mountaineers, 73–74; for southern blacks, 89–90, 92, 99–101, 109–11, 117
Urbanization, 3, 8, 10, 44, 46

Virginia: Baptist orphanage in, 59; mountain schools in, 81, 83; Fortress Monroe, 92, 94
Volunteerism, 20

Washington, Booker T., 109
Webb, W. S., 49
Wheeler, Edward L., 92, 110
White, John E., 74, 78, 81
Williamson, Joel, 12, 90–91, 103, 115
Wilson, Charles Reagan, 113–14
Wilson, M. A., 80
Winkler, E. T., 92–93
Woodward, C. Vann, 1

Yancey Collegiate Institute, 85, 121

ABOUT THE AUTHOR

Keith Harper is Assistant Professor of Church History at Southeastern Baptist Theological Seminary, Wake Forest, North Carolina. He received his bachelor's degree from Lexington Baptist College, his master's from Murray State University, and his doctorate from the University of Kentucky.